The

ourage to
hange

The  ourage to hange

Stories From Successful School Reform

Paul E. Heckman
Teachers and the Principal
at Ochoa Elementary School
Relate Their Experiences

CORWIN PRESS, INC.
A Sage Publications Company
Thousand Oaks, California

For information address:

Corwin Press, Inc.
A Sage Publications Company
2455 Teller Road
Thousand Oaks, California 91320
E-mail: order@corwin.sagepub.com

SAGE Publications Ltd.
6 Bonhill Street
London EC2A 4PU
United Kingdom

SAGE Publications India Pvt. Ltd.
M-32 Market
Greater Kailash I
New Delhi 110 048 India

Printed in the United States of America

Library of Congress Cataloging-in-Publication Data

Heckman, Paul E.
    The courage to change: Stories from successful school reform /
Paul E. Heckman
        p. cm.
    Includes bibliographical references.
    ISBN 0-8039-6329-7 (cloth: alk. paper). — ISBN 0-8039-6330-0
(paper: alk. paper)
        1. Educational change—Arizona—Tucson—Case studies.   2. Action
research in education—Arizona—Tucson—Case studies.   3. School
management and organization—Arizona—Tucson—Case studies.
    I. Title.
    LA239-T84H43 1995
    370'.9791'776—dc20   95–30791

This book is printed on acid-free paper.

96 97 98 99 10 9 8 7 6 5 4 3 2 1

Production Editor: Gillian Dickens   Typesetter: Christina M. Hill

Contents

Foreword

Anyone burdened with knowledge of my writings on school change will know that I do not regard that arena optimistically, let alone with great expectations. The reasons are many, not the least of which is the most unrealistic time perspective that the schools' changers adopt. The self-defeating nature of that time perspective only becomes evident when the predictable problems of school change are encountered in the process of implementation. It is then that the fan blows other than air and failure appears on the horizon.

I say "predictable problems" advisedly because in too many of the instances I have observed (or read or know about), those problems should and could have been anticipated. This does not mean, of course, that if those problems had been known, the course of the change process would have had smooth sailing. That is never the case in complicated human affairs, and changing schools is a very complicated affair. So, for example, there was a time not too long ago when people believed that an infusion of money into schools would bring about desired changes. No one believes that anymore. It was an understandable but egregiously oversimple expectation. And then there were (and still are) efforts based on what I call the "shape up or ship out" ideology: raise standards, sustain and maintain them, emphasize the "basics," de-emphasize "frills," and all good things will follow. Supporting evidence is a tiny bit above nil, if at all.

And what about the turbulent sixties, when the answer to school inadequacies was the new math, the new physics, the new biology, and the new social studies? That was a disaster instigated (with the best intentions) by academics whose understanding of the culture of schools was as sophisticated as is mine of Eskimo culture.

Today we are told about the wonders of site-based management, a concept with which I agree, except that its substance and implications are hardly spelled out so that, in practice, it is less a concept than an inkblot. In the instances of which I have direct knowledge, site-based management *in practice* is at best a token gesture and at worst a sheer mockery. And in all of these instances the predictable problems were ignored or glossed over.

Then why, in light of the above, did I agree 5 years ago to observe Dr. Paul Heckman's school change project in Tucson, Arizona? And why have I continued to visit it twice a year? The answer to the first question is that I was intrigued by Dr. Heckman's rationale that the task for him and his colleagues was to interconnect and to enable neighborhood, community, and school personnel to come up with *their* conception of the school they wanted and could agree on. The first school was in a very poor, almost exclusively Latino-populated area. It was *not* the obligation or task of the research group to tell them how to think and act; that is, they were not in the role of the outside expert coming in with a preconceived plan they sought to "sell," to bring, so to speak, culture to the primitives. That rationale intrigued me because it reflected a view of empowerment that made sense in that it suggested that a school "psychologically owned" by these individuals and groups could expect from them a degree of motivation and commitment that would help garner the appropriate resources and probably ensure a consistency between intentions and actions. If it made sense to me, it also aroused my concern that Dr. Heckman was underestimating the difficulties he would encounter.

That first visit to Ochoa Elementary School was inspiring to me and, I confess, surprising. There were difficulties, predictable and unpredictable. But it appeared that most of them were being confronted and surmounted, which is why I have continued to visit the school twice a year.

In this first book about the project, we are given the experience of school personnel: their initial misgivings, the *Sturm und Drang* of personal and institutional change, their persistence, and much more.

It was a wise decision that the first book be the stories of teachers, because they make it clear that the quality and strength of their motivation, the manifestations of their creativity and willingness to take risks, to depart from stultifying convention, crucially depended on an ambiance and ethos they had heretofore not experienced.

Generally speaking, teachers, like the rest of us, resist change. Where we go wrong is in concluding that the resistance is an individual characteristic, as if the person, so to speak, has an encapsulated place in his or her personality/intellectual makeup containing the tendency to oppose, resist, or even subvert change. That, of course, is nonsense because it ignores the ever-present role of context on how or when any person expresses thought and feeling in action. Given the cultures of schools, teachers have good reason to be wary of changes people seek to get them to make.

In this book, what teachers willingly and candidly report is incomprehensible apart from the fact that the conditions freeing them to think in new and sometimes risky ways, and to take responsibility for their actions, individually and collectively, had been created. That should be obvious, but too few people take the obvious seriously. Dr. Heckman took the obvious seriously, which is why the teachers, who coauthored this book, have made an important contribution to all of us.

I spoke earlier and critically about the time perspective of those seeking to change schools in this or that way. I want to congratulate the foundations supporting Dr. Heckman's efforts for comprehending that his rationale required a time perspective that realistically mirrored the complexities and perplexities of comprehensive school change. It is rare indeed for funding sources to support a project where it was impossible to state ahead of time when—if ever—the minimal conditions for that kind of change would become evident. School change is not, like building a bridge, a matter of engineering. If it were, changing schools would not be the national concern it is.

Seymour B. Sarason
Yale University

Acknowledgments

The families of the Ochoa Elementary School children deserve much credit for their interest and perseverance in seeking educational opportunities that benefit their children. We also acknowledge the wonderful children and the spirit with which they accepted many changes in their school during the past 5 years.

The project was launched in 1990 with the encouragement of Dr. Paul Houston, then superintendent of the Tucson Unified School District (TUSD) and now executive director of the American Association of School Administrators. The TUSD-ECC Project collaboration continued with Dr. Houston's successor, Dr. George Garcia, to whom we are especially indebted for supporting our work. If the project can claim a "guardian angel," it is Elaine Rice, TUSD assistant superintendent, who continues to stick by us through thick and thin, tribulation and triumph. We also are grateful for the support of the University of Arizona, especially Dr. John Taylor, dean of the College of Education.

Both financial and moral support has been provided by a wonderful group of foundations and foundation representatives. Dr. Pat Edwards, program officer of the Charles Stewart Mott Foundation, shepherded the project's initial proposal through the Mott Foundation in 1990, and since that time has contacted other funding partners and generally urged all of us forward. Other funding sources provided invaluable support, including The Pew Charitable Trusts, with education director Robert Schwartz and program officer Lallie O'Brien providing very able and thoughtful attention to the project. Finally, the Carnegie Foundation, with program officer Michael Levine, provided a small, yet important, grant to promote the development of new assessment practices in project schools.

These foundations shared in funding the project's competent board of consultants, which includes Drs. Edwards, Eugene Garcia, Luis Moll, Donna Muncey, Susana Navarro, Jeannie Oakes, and Seymour Sarason. We wish further to acknowledge the contribution of the late Dr. Edward Meade. We are very grateful for the thoughtful support of Dr. Sarason, who wrote the foreword for this book, and Dr. Oakes, chairman of the board, both of whom have been strong advocates of the project since its beginning. Also, we are especially appreciative of Dr. Angela Covert and Jacqueline Danzberger, whose guidance and attention to the project have been invaluable. Title 1 director Patricia Lopez and project specialist Carol Brooks also have provided encouragement in the use of Title 1 resources in support of ECC Project efforts.

We would be remiss if we didn't acknowledge the site-based staff membrs who have worked as "third-party" participants with the faculty at Ochoa Elementary School and the residents of South Tucson, where Ochoa is located. At the close of the fifth school year, that staff included the project coordinator, Viki Montera, who has supported the project since its inception; Anna Loebe, Hilda Angiulo, and Kyle Shanton, site coordinators; and Jean Peacock, who has served as both community coordinator and site coordinator during her 4 years with the project. Office support comes from the administrative associate, Julia Acedo, who guards the coffers and keeps our expenditures in line; Sally Showalter, who does the nitty-gritty of guest teacher arrangements; and Irma Barragan, the secretary who keeps track of where each of us is at any given hour.

Finally, we say "thank you" to Bobbie Justice, editor and writer for the ECC Project, who worked her magic on the many paragraphs that each of us wrote. She coaxed better phrases and additional details and stories from each of us in a firm and loving fashion as she herded all of the writers in one direction toward the book's finale. She also has shown the power of creativity by taking the germ of an idea and promoting it into what this book has become.

About the Authors

Paul E. Heckman is Associate Professor in the Teaching and Teacher Education Department of the College of Education at the University of Arizona and has been principal investigator of the Educational and Community Change Project since he conceived the project in 1990. He was born in New Jersey and is a graduate of The King's College, Briarcliff Manor, New York. He received his master's degree from Boston University and was a middle-school teacher and school administrator in New Hampshire before moving to Los Angeles, where he taught elementary school and earned his Ph.D. from the University of California, Los Angeles, in 1982. Since that time, his academic and research efforts have been focused on school restructuring and curricular change through university-school partnerships at UCLA, at the University of Southern Maine, and at the University of Arizona, where, in 1987, he became an assistant dean in the College of Education and executive director of the Tucson School-University Partnership.

Ana Maria Andrade, a native of Tucson, has been in the field of education since 1965, when she joined the Tucson Unified School

District (TUSD) as an instructional aide in an elementary school. In 1974 she earned an associate arts degree in early childhood education at Pima Community College and later a bachelor of arts degree in elementary education at the University of Arizona, where she finished with a bilingual endorsement. She became a bilingual team teacher of first grade and continued her studies at the University of Arizona, earning her master of arts degree in bilingual education in 1987. At that time she became a Title 1 bilingual resource teacher at Ochoa Elementary School and was later certified as a reading recovery teacher. In seeing changes that were taking place in the classrooms at Ochoa, she determined in 1993 that she wanted a class of her own, rather than continuing as a resource teacher. She feels her team-teaching experience between 1978 and 1987 is helpful in the work that she does now at Ochoa, and she has had considerable experience working with Spanish-speaking parents.

Suzanne (Sue) Bishop was born in Merced, California, and is a graduate of the University of California/Santa Barbara. She describes herself as being "from a teaching family," referring to her mother, father, and two sisters, who are educators, and her husband, who taught government in high school and who now works with prospective teachers. Most of her 20 years as an educator have been in Title 1 reading (pull-out), Higher Order Thinking Skills (computer lab), and in-class model resource teaching. She joined the Ochoa faculty in 1967 and says she finds teaching in a multicultural school very interesting. Furthermore, she prefers teaching in communities that are less than affluent, because "the students are warm and appreciative," and she feels she can make a difference in their lives. Although her favorite age group is third grade, she says she is enjoying team-teaching intermediate students in the ECC Project school.

Marianne Chavez was born in Fort Campbell, Kentucky. She describes her early school experiences as "having a rough time," because her first language was Spanish, and she recalls being ridiculed or punished many times when she was caught speaking Spanish at school. By the age of 8 she knew she wanted to be a teacher, and her role model was a fourth-grade teacher named Mrs. Warfield, whom Chavez describes as loving and sensitive to students' needs and the first teacher who "accepted me the way I was."

She is one of 15 children, and she and one of her sisters (a nurse) are the only children in the family to earn college degrees, both from the University of Arizona. She has taught off and on for about 9 years, although she held various other positions in the school district for 15 years. She finds it exciting to learn about other cultures in a multicultural school and says her heart is where children and their families are very needy: "I feel I can make a difference for them." As to the multilingual teaching that is going on at Ochoa school, she says she wishes she had been taught in both languages.

Christine (Chris) B. Confer moved to Tucson from Euclid, Ohio, shortly after she was born, so she considers herself a "near" native of the Southwest. She earned a bachelor's degree with a bilingual endorsement and master of arts in reading from the University of Arizona. Seventeen years ago, she became a teacher at Ochoa Elementary School. Four years later she became a Title 1 reading resource teacher, first at another school and then returning in that capacity to Ochoa. She continues in the Title 1 program today as a math/science instructional support teacher at Ochoa and works with all of the teachers, as well as all of the children—from 4-year-olds to fifth-graders. She has always taught in multicultural schools and says her awareness of the discrepancy between the incredible abilities of children in low socioeconomic areas and their traditional lack of success in schools challenges her. Her goal is to find ways to change schooling and provide greater access for children in low socioeconomic areas.

Laura C. Fahr is a native of Tucson. After receiving her bachelor's degree from Arizona State University she did graduate work at the University of Arizona. She has been a teacher for 24 years, 14 of which have been at Ochoa. She prefers teaching in a multicultural school because she grew up with cultural diversity and always appreciated the Mexican and Native American cultures. "It's 'home' for me—a natural environment," she says. She also prefers teaching in poorer communities and considers it more of a challenge. She says she feels that what poor children do not have in tangible things they make up for in other ways, but it is a joy to expose these children to things they have not had or seen. As a native of Tucson, she has always known some Spanish; however, several years ago she spent several months tutoring in Italy and feels she had a tendency to lose some of the Spanish (and Latin) she knew before that time. Although she has always been interested in and taught intermediate grades, readers will find she is very enthusiastic about multiage/grade teaching.

Delia C. Hakim, whose first language is Spanish, is a native of Tucson and finished high school in one of the Tucson school districts. Her teaching career began in 1971, when she received her bachelor of arts degree from the University of Arizona, and she later earned her master's degree in counseling and guidance from that university. She has taught both primary and intermediate grades in California as well as in Arizona, and has been at Ochoa Elementary School for 14 years. Before becoming a participant in the Educational and Community Change Project 4 years ago, her primary responsibility at Ochoa was the first grade. Since that time, she has been involved in multiage groupings of classes that combine fifth-graders with first-graders, and she team-teaches first-grade classes that include Spanish-dominant and English-dominant students. She has a keen interest in languages and cultures and in 1993 obtained a bilingual teaching endorsement.

Linda S. Ketcham was born and raised in Tucson and received her public education in the same school district in which she is teaching. She has a bicultural background; her mother is Anglo, and her stepfather is a Digueño Indian from Southern California. She earned her bachelor's degree from the University of Arizona, and has been a teacher at Ochoa for 8 years, the first 4 of which she taught fourth grade. She was among the first teachers at Ochoa to try team-teaching, when she combined her English-speaking fourth-grade class with a Spanish-dominant fourth-grade class. She later team-taught with two other teachers an ungraded intermediate class of fourth, fifth, and sixth grades. At the beginning of the 1994-1995 school year, a district realignment brought about her transfer out of Ochoa to a magnet middle school, where she continues to use some of the practices she developed during her years in the ECC Project at Ochoa.

Elsa N. Padilla, a graduate of the University of Arizona, was born in Guines, Havana, Cuba. At the age of 15, she moved with her family to the United States, where she was inspired to pursue a career in education by a teacher in her first class: a special education class for non-English-speaking recent arrivals in the United States. She has worked in a bilingual, multicultural setting for 23 years, including 8 ½ years as a special education resource teacher, 2 years as a special education program specialist, and 5 ½ years as Assistant Director of Special Education. In 1989 she became principal at Ochoa Elementary School, where she feels her bilingual, bicultural background is an asset in various ways, especially in helping parents and students connect to schooling: "I feel I can be a true advocate of students and parents."

Rebecca (Becky) Romero was born in Cananea, Sonora, Mexico, and moved with her family to Tucson at a very early age. She is a graduate of the University of Arizona, where she also earned her master's degree in teaching and teacher education. She has been teaching preschool and elementary school students for 11 years, nearly all of those years at Ochoa School. Before becoming a participant in the ECC Project, she taught second grade and is now teamed with Marianne Chavez in a multiage grouping of second- and third-graders. Her introduction to teaching was in the Parent and Child Education (PACE) program. She has a special interest in working with primary and younger children and prefers teaching in multicultural schools because they provide an opportunity to study—and learn from—diverse cultures.

Introduction

The chapters that follow describe the development of individuals and a school that are involved in an action research effort known as The Educational and Community Change (ECC) Project. We, the authors, believe the stories told in this book will make a unique contribution to the literature about school reform, because much of its content is written by the teachers and principal who have been—and still are—on the front lines. They are among the individuals most involved in the project's efforts to reinvent education; they are workers and voices for change in their classroom practices and their school's structures.

Often projects with goals similar to those of the ECC Project treat teachers, parents, and principals simply as subjects that are undergoing a "treatment" to manifest prescribed results, and books about these reform efforts simply present what happened with the treatment and its development. In this book, the reader will experience "indigenous invention," a process in which the individuals most involved in the change effort (teachers, principal, parents, and so on) are the key to what will or will not be accomplished in the classrooms, the school, and the community. We believe that when particular conditions are created anew, individuals, such as the writers in this volume, will be propelled to reinvent their ideas and conceptions of schooling, including the work they do as teachers and principal, as well as the work children do in their classrooms. Very little, if any, ECC Project work is done by prescription.

To ward off questions that may later arise among readers, I want to say a word about the issue of the teachers' union and the project. A democratic perspective has served as part of the foundation of the ECC Project since its inception. Such a perspective urges full and equal participation by all of those involved. Participants don't do anything that they do not wish to do. Each individual teacher decides or does not decide to participate in project activities and in changing ideas and practices at the school. Hence, I did not believe a nego- tiated agreement between the teachers' union and the project was necessary. The project would neither coerce nor encourage any teacher to do what he or she did not want to do within the boundaries of the negotiated district and union contract. A provision in the agreement does allow an entire faculty to take an action contrary to the agreement if all of the teachers decide together to do that. During the past 5 years, neither the district nor I have had to deal with any grievance filed against the project or its activities.

During this time period, some teachers have participated in project activities and then taken some time off, varying from several meetings to several months. Several teachers have participated on and off during the years and have now decided that they do not at this time want to further involve themselves. Elsa Padilla, the principal, will further discuss this issue in Chapter 11. She will explore from her perspective what has happened with those who sometimes view themselves as in and with those who occasionally see themselves as out.

Before offering further insights about the project's "school re- invention" work, I want to provide a context in which the reader can place the teachers' stories:

The Tucson Unified School District (TUSD) has 105 schools and serves 65,000 children and youths in Tucson, Arizona, and Pima County. Situated within Tucson is the City of South Tucson, it is a 1-square-mile urban area that is populated primarily by Latinos and Native Americans. About 55% of the families in that area live at, or below, the poverty level, and three fourths of the persons over the age of 18 do not possess a high school diploma or GED. There are two elementary schools in the City of South Tucson, one of which is Ochoa, the school on which this book focuses.

With the cooperation of administrators in the TUSD, Ochoa was selected, in the fall of 1990, as the first school to become involved in the ECC Project. At that time, 385 students attended the school; there were 16 certified teachers, 5 Title 1 (at that time called Chapter 1, but referred to throughout this book as Title 1) resource teachers, and 12 teaching assistants.

Ninety percent of Ochoa students were Latino and 10% were Native American. Sixty-five percent of the Latino students had arrived in the United States during the previous 3 years, and although some students spoke English, Spanish was the primary language of most. Because 95% of the students were eligible for free lunches, the school received funds from the Elementary and Secondary Education Act's (ESEA) Title I and Title VII, as well as state categorical funds to assist in the education of economically poor children. This enrollment profile fit well with the project's primary objective to explore conditions that are necessary if change is to occur and education is to be reinvented for children of color in low-income areas.

The ECC Project's rationale for a new set of educational conditions in schools focuses on the belief that many of the ideas underlying existing schooling practices and structures were created nearly 100 years ago, when reformers were creating schools for the Industrial Age. The Industrial Age has passed, yet those century-old ideas, practices, and structures remain in our schools today, creating negative consequences to children who are economically poor, are of color, and whose primary language is other than English. For example, economically poor Latino children in the United States drop out of school at the rate of about 65%, despite local, state, and national efforts to alter this pattern. In a similar fashion, 90% of Native American children and youths drop out of school. These trends exist in Tucson, and state and local district programs appear to be unsuccessful in attenuating these rates.

Consequently, in 1990, I requested a 5-year grant from the Charles Stewart Mott Foundation to reinvent education in an elementary school in the City of South Tucson. Funds from the Mott Foundation were matched by other funding sources, and later The Pew Charitable Trusts joined in funding the project's efforts. At the time of this writing, the project is in two elementary schools, and funds have been extended for an additional 3 years to accommodate not only expansion of the project to additional schools but also the beginning of an assessment process for the work being done.

Many conditions at Ochoa have changed and are changing, yet there is no end to successful reform. In the chapters that follow, the reader will "visit" with eight of the teachers and the principal at Ochoa who are among the school's participants in the project.

In Chapter 1 of this book, the goals of the project and the preconditions that were requested from the school staff are examined, and teachers describe their expectations and anxieties in embarking on a totally undefined way of teaching. Changes were to be made, but not by legislation or district edict; they, the teachers and principal, were to conceive and implement the changes.

The heart of the ECC Project is dialogue—intense, self-revealing dialogue sessions in which teachers examine, in depth, their beliefs and ideas about schooling. Chapter 2 reveals the benefits of dialogue as well as the "hurts" that can be felt in self-examination and disclosure to colleagues of one's true beliefs.

Teaching is said to be a lonely profession. Through dialogue and participation in the project, teachers at Ochoa found they did not have to be closeted in their classrooms, and soon they began to work in teams. There is no departmentalization in the teaming; instead, two or more teachers assume responsibility for the same group of students. In Chapter 3, teachers define their teaming experiences, both good and bad.

Team teaching was an important factor when it was decided to discontinue the practice of language tracking at Ochoa. Today, Ochoa teachers recognize a language other than English as an asset, and efforts focus on children becoming bilingual by the time they leave elementary school. Teacher-teams simultaneously teach classes in English and Spanish, and Chapter 4 reveals many of the expected and unexpected results of mixing the Spanish-dominant and English-dominant children.

Team teaching also appears to be the impetus for teachers deciding to mix classes of various age groups. Thus, they began trying a variety of mixes during certain segments of the school day. There were surprising results of interaction in allowing a mixed class of fourth-, fifth-, and sixth-graders to teach chess to a class of 6-year-olds (first-graders). More permanent mixes of age groups have now been established at Ochoa, as revealed in Chapter 5. The mix of age groups also provides an opportunity for teachers to work with students longer and to build interest and confidence in parents, because teachers often are with the same students for 2 or 3 years.

Some students from economically poor neighborhoods or cultures other than Anglo appear to have difficulty relating to much of the knowledge they are expected to acquire in traditional, textbook schooling. Chapter 6 describes and pinpoints the value of contextualized units of study that are meaningful to the young learners. Many of the lessons are conceived through the process of inquiry, with questions initiated by the students as well as the teachers. It's a process of building on the knowledge children already have when they come to school.

Student behavior is an issue in nearly every school and area in the country today. There's no single answer, and in Chapter 7, teachers point out that elimination of inappropriate behavior is a difficult task; however, engaging the interest and curiosity of children at Ochoa has been an important step in the improvement of students' actions in the classrooms. Many conflicts are resolved by the students themselves through teachers' efforts in encouraging children to be responsible for their own behavior and the behavior of their classmates.

When textbooks and lesson plans are no longer the ritual of schooling, creativity must be expanded by both the teachers and the students. Creativity is a major part of the ECC Project's belief in indigenous invention. The sole responsibility of a child's education does not rest on the teachers and the principal of a school. The child must play a major role, as must the parents and members of the child's community. Chapter 8 reveals how some of the responsibilities of education are being shared by all.

The Project has completed its fifth year, and work in the next 3 years will begin to focus on alternative assessment practices to complement the alternative teaching and learning practices that are taking place at Ochoa. In Chapter 9, teachers discuss ways they believe may help in assessing the value of the education they are providing for the children. One way includes the teachers' self-assessment of what they are offering their students in knowledge and skills, especially in problem finding and problem solving.

Literature continues to emphasize the importance of parents, guardians, and other family members taking part in a child's education. In Chapter 10, teachers describe methods for bringing parents into their classroom activities and establishing personal relationships with parents through various means of communication.

Very few goals are met without strong supportive leadership, and that leadership within a school such as Ochoa must come from the principal. Principals are called upon to do a great deal of self-examination and risk taking if education reform is to be effective. Although mentioned in many places throughout the book, Elsa Padilla, the principal at Ochoa, reveals in Chapter 11 her beliefs of the past and the present and describes the "right stuff" needed by a principal engaged in change.

Finally, each of us sums up in Chapter 12 where we've been, where we are, where we hope we are going. It is evident throughout the book that many changes have occurred in Ochoa School and in the students and parents. These changes would not have occurred if the teachers had not changed. Perhaps there will be inspiration here for teachers and other educators, school districts, and legislative bodies to examine the benefits of a change effort such as the ECC Project.

Paul E. Heckman
Principal Investigator

1

Exploring Conditions
for Change

Participation in the ECC Project was a voluntary thing. Upon hearing the goals advanced and the commitments required, teachers were enthusiastic about breaking the bonds of traditional practices that appeared to have been detrimental in educating the children in this low-economic, primarily Latino neighborhood. There was consensus among the teachers that the school would participate in the project, yet there was considerable skepticism about underlying motives of the research staff and anxiety about embarking on a totally uncharted course on which they themselves would be the navigators.

The Educational and Community Change (ECC) Project focuses on conditions that are necessary to bring about school change. However, before the project became a reality, there were certain preconditions that had to be agreed upon by teachers and the principal at Ochoa Elementary School as well as the Tucson Unified School District, ECC Project funders, and the project staff.

The first of the preconditions was adherence to goals of the project:

1. to improve dramatically the achievement of students in mathematics, science, social science, literature, the arts, reading, and writing;
2. to restructure schooling practices so that poor and minority students achieve well beyond elementary schools, and thus the dropout rate diminishes; and
3. to develop assessment and evaluation practices that more accurately convey how much children have achieved in this alternative school project.

These goals were important to me for several reasons. First, I did not have an interest in just any school change and had no interest in promoting school change for the sake of school change. Rather, the invention of education must have purposes and intentions. These goals reveal the intentions of the ECC Project and the sense of what will receive attention.

Public schools have an explicit belief about the importance of student achievement in the subject fields (i.e., mathematics, science, reading, etc.); however, when educators, children, and parents see the subject fields only as a collection of factoids to be acquired, all students will have difficulty achieving in these areas.

The ECC Project shares the belief that students must achieve in the subject fields, but, in addition, it seeks more powerful ideas about what achievement in each of these subject fields might be, so that all poor and minority children might achieve in these areas. I believed at the outset of the project, and even more so now after 5 years, that promoting ways of thinking as a scientist, mathematician, and the like has importance for promoting student achievement in each of these areas. When children can be scientists and do the work of scientists and so forth, they will be engaged and can acquire the ways of thinking in each subject field area.

The second goal of the project relates to the first. As students achieve in these new ways as scientists and such, both short-term and long-term consequences must accrue to them, or else these changes will not have justification. The short-term consequences have to do with success later in schooling and staying in school to complete high school and college. Any change in the educational system has to address the underlying causes for the staggering levels of dropout rates in this country, especially among Latino and Native American children.

With regard to the final goal, existing assessment and achievement measures seek differentiation between the high and low "achievers," rather than promoting ways for children to reveal what they know and for the public to see the products of this knowledge.

In sum, then, the goals of the project and the acceptance of them as preconditions of participation in the project's development required the acknowledgment that an entire set of activities and practices of education had to be examined and altered at the same time, not just one or two aspects of education.

The second precondition involved a commitment to an adequate time frame for accomplishing significant reinvention at the school. (That initial time frame was 5 years, but subsequently it was extended to 8.) To unpack and alter the century-old ideas and beliefs that underlie existing schooling practices and structures and create new ones based on new ideas would take time—if, indeed, it could be accomplished. Commitment to the long time frame became a precondition but there was a default clause: At any point in time, participants at the school could drop out of the process. The default clause seemed important for two reasons: (a) Few projects have taken this long-term perspective, and I did not know what would happen to either my interests in such intense work or the interests of those who would do most of the hardest work; and (b) given the voluntary nature of this activity (anyone could stop and start his or her participation at any time), the possibility existed that at some point in the future, many—if not all—might stop their participation.

A third precondition was the necessity that every aspect of the ideas underlying existing practices and structures would be examined, and, on the part of the project, time would be allowed during the teachers' workweek for them to convene in dialogue sessions that would facilitate examination and change. Each aspect of a school has to be seen as connected to other parts. If one part changes, the symmetry of schooling will be off. To restore the symmetry, other parts will have to be altered or the change will have to be eliminated, which has happened more often than not in the history of school reform in the United States. The project acknowledged that if important changes are to be made, the reinvention work must occur during the workday and week and teachers must have focused time to examine existing beliefs and practices and create them anew. Thus, teachers would have a predetermined time during their work-week to focus on change and reinvention.

Perhaps the most important of the preconditions was the accep-tance that changes would be created as well as implemented by the participants and not by outside parties; project staff would work alongside as third-party participants—contributing and facilitat-ing—but not directing. Acceptance of this precondition highlights a major difference of this project from many others. For participants in the project, what happened at the school remained at the school and neighborhood level with those most affected by whatever they together decided to do.

These preconditions were accepted by the participating teachers, and the project work was under way in the fall of 1990.

Although this book is not in chronological order, let's begin with the first year and explore what was understood about the Ochoa teachers and principal being the individuals who would establish conditions to create changes. Understandably, at the beginning of the project, teachers did not easily differentiate between the task of *creating and developing* the conditions for change and *implementing* particular changes developed by others outside the school. Addi-tional confusion existed between the use of project funds to establish conditions for teachers to create their own innovations and that of purchasing new curriculum and instructional materials to be used (implemented) in their classrooms.

Such confusion derives from a prevailing ideology of educational and curriculum change in the United States and, no doubt, in all developed industrialized countries. In particular, classrooms and schools have existed in a society in which the economy has a strong industrial basis, and the public and private institutions are governed according to bureaucratic principles. This history and these princi-ples encouraged teachers and other educators to accept the idea that they are to implement innovations presented to them by those in the school district (or state or federal governing bodies) who have higher positions of authority and/or whose roles involve creating innova-tions for teachers (workers) to implement. The acceptance of these ideas makes it more difficult for teachers and others to differentiate between an ideology of "implementation of innovation" and one we refer to in the ECC Project as "indigenous invention."

Let's consider an analogy of the situation: School and district administrators and policymakers have seen teachers—and teachers have long seen themselves—as workers on a production line, teaching particular knowledge and skills to a particular group of students of the same grade level (usually the same age). There are similarities to an assembly line in the specified pieces of work for each grade level and the tasks performed by the line worker who does a particular process or puts a part on a to-be-completed product.

Students have similarities to production-line products. When the product (a student) has completely moved down the line, he or she will have had parts added and finishing processes done so that the product exits the line finished. In fact, a completely assembled product will have little variance from any other product made on this or any other production line making a similar product. The variances will stay within an acceptable range of prescribed standards for this product.

At Ochoa, as at most other schools, the workers on the assembly line historically have had little to say about the design of the product and the assembly line, including the tasks and the time frame for completing the tasks in making the product. These workers have even less influence on the standards of excellence. Generally, management and others in the organization have the specific functions of designing products and manufacturing processes and deciding on the product, manufacturing tasks, time frame for completing the tasks, and the standards.

The ECC Project's focus on indigenous invention contrasts sharply with the ideas of implementation of innovation, industrialization, and bureaucratization. As the word *indigenous* suggests, local individuals do the inventing. Those individuals, in the case of school change, are teachers, principals, parents, and sometimes the students. These local people create or invent new ideas and practices and then put them into action (implement).

At Ochoa School, inquiry and examination of every aspect of what anyone did and thought in classrooms became a primary condition for promoting indigenous invention at the beginning of the project and continuing to this day. Every participant questions what was never questioned in the past. Raising these questions does not imply that anyone does or did anything wrong; instead, skepticism prevails about everything that goes on—and went on—in the school and the ideas that support(ed) such practices and structures. Chris Confer and Marianne Chavez provide illustrative suggestions in this chapter of what they and their colleagues began to question: grouping structures, how classroom decisions were made, what to learn, how to evaluate the learning and activities, and the relationships among parents, teachers, administrators, and the larger community.

As Delia Hakim suggests in this chapter, such examination and inquiry require courage—courage to question and override the anxiety that arises as one questions what has seemed so normal. Ambiguity increased significantly, as did anxiety, as teachers questioned and examined at the same time many aspects of schooling and realized they were to create heretofore unknown changes. As the stories unfold, the obvious emotional aspects of change, especially the ambiguous character of these changes, receive a lot of attention in this and other chapters, as they should. These emotional aspects of school change go often unreported and unanalyzed in the change literature. Psychologist Rollo May titled one of his books *The Courage to Create*. This chapter and others to follow highlight the courage that invention requires and that these teachers and the principal exhibited in successfully altering many of their ideas and addressing the emotions that resulted.

DELIA: In the very beginning, I had a lot of questions. I wondered how it was going to work, but I imagined that there would be an organized plan, which we teachers could take and simply put into action. After all, that was the way schools always did things. Somebody in the world (usually not a teacher) would conceive a new way of teaching, and teachers would then implement the "great ideas" of that "somebody."

I thought too that the district administration was somehow involved in the preplanning of the project and that our school was going to be a totally experimental school, operating without the traditional bureaucracy.

I had thought that all of the teachers would be eager to participate—that, given the opportunity to make innovative changes, they would all want to participate in every part of the project.

I also thought that the teachers in the project could just let go and put new ideas into action immediately. And all of our own creative ideas, which in the past we didn't want anyone to really know about for fear of being labeled "different," could be introduced in the classroom.

I soon learned I was wrong on virtually all counts. There was no prepackaged plan, and the administration was not involved in the "workings" of the project. Though there was consensus among the teachers to participate in the project, not all of them chose to participate in all aspects of the project. (It was somewhat like results of the Emancipation Proclamation, when not all of the slaves chose freedom.) Furthermore, it would be quite a long time before any of our creative ideas could be implemented.

Paul Heckman, a professor from the University of Arizona and principal investigator for this trial-balloon venture, and several university graduate students met with those of us who had volunteered for the project. Some of us were scared to run the risk of change, but we knew there was something better out there—a better way to teach our kids. We didn't know how to do it, but we knew in our hearts there was a better way.

BECKY: I'm an Early Childhood person; my background was primarily with preschoolers and PACE (Parent and Child Education). I believe in hands-on teaching, which is what I thought the project people were suggesting. I always felt that other teachers should do more hands-on instruction, instead of doing workbooks, ditto sheets, and that kind of thing. Children learn by being able to touch, but after they get to a certain grade level— high school—it's listening to lectures, taking notes, reading books, answering questions. I've often wondered if developmentally somewhere along the line someone said: "By the time kids reach a certain age they don't need the hands-on stuff anymore." I hoped that the Educational and Community Change Project would change all of that.

I had continued to offer my second- and third-grade students hands-on learning, because I continued to keep the same ideas about how children learn. I knew that kids had to be encouraged and I thought my classroom was already very much like what the project people were suggesting. At the very beginning, I was scared of the project, frightened of the whole idea of change, but I went along with it just to see. Actually, I thought the way I ran my class was really right.

Later I realized there were quite a few things that I needed to change; for instance, allowing kids more choice, giving them the opportunity to figure things out for themselves. I know a lot of us teachers are guilty of giving kids the answers instead of making it possible for them to figure the answer out for themselves. The children would ask questions and right away I would give them the answers. This was the kind of practice I needed to change.

LINDA: The principal had asked us if we'd like to pursue this project, and I can remember wondering what the university people were going to get out of all this. In fact, I asked the ECC Project's principal investigator, Paul Heckman, and he said he wasn't getting anything out of it, that he had his regular job at the university in addition to this project.

I knew that someone higher up than myself had to grant permission for us to even entertain the idea of changing school. I saw the whole school system, the school district and its policies and rules, as the biggest obstacles to change. When we met as a faculty with Paul he asked us, "What needs to change to make school better for children?" In a way that seemed to be a form of permission, and I became very optimistic about the project. For so many years I had heard people say, "Public education is this and that and is failing our kids." And now someone was saying that we had a chance to do something about it—to change, to do something different, to address the problems that people were complaining about. It was my hope that we could change things—and I would learn something from this process.

Very early in my teaching career I developed a desire to "do right by my kids," even if it meant straying some from adopted materials. This project enhanced my motivation, and I embraced this proposal for change.

SUE: When Paul Heckman first introduced the project to us, it seemed like a dream come true. We all have so much concern for the children at Ochoa. Now there was a chance to create a place where children were not only safe, but felt love and acceptance and could grow to their fullest potential. What a wonderful dream! The talk of thousands of dollars to support the project brought images of "more"—more field trips, more equipment, more beautiful books to share with the children.

That was my dream. In reality, however, I was skeptical even of this very warm and caring man whose gentle talk held so much promise. And so, in the beginning, I sat and watched.

LAURA: I kept thinking there had to be an ulterior motive, that the project's principal investigator had to have his own thing that was going to come out of this, but I didn't have a basis for distrusting him. At the same time, I was immediately enthralled with the idea of using new methods in math education. I had already begun to see math education as an active, involving process, not the memorization of algorithms and numbers. I had begun to read more professionally and had a more active interest in what was said by the Secretary of Education and the President and in people's reactions to test scores and comments about how badly we were educating the kids.

For at least 5 years I had found it painful to watch the change in kids, their attitudes, the lack of values that parents were providing for education. Parents saw school as just a place to send kids, and the kids saw it that way too. Kids had already changed to the extent that you couldn't "make" them do anything. You couldn't "make" them memorize multiplication tables; you couldn't "make" them do homework.

So when the principal offered the ECC Project, it was a real turning point. I remember being excited, because we would be on-site in terms of curriculum changes and approaches to things. And I loved the fact that the principal was so receptive and responsive to things and encouraged us in risk taking.

I kept thinking the project's director had to have an agenda, and he kept assuring us he didn't. The ideas were up to us, and we had permission to explore them. That whole thing was so foreign and so totally unknown in education; we had always been driven by textbooks, curriculum guides, and district directives.

Marianne was already under the pressure of changing the direction of her career at the time the project was getting under way. She was just getting back into the teaching practices she had used in her earlier days of teaching and, at first, was reluctant to take on something new.

MARIANNE: When the project was introduced in 1990 and Ochoa teachers were considering participation in the project, I was a program specialist for the school district and had been away from classroom teaching for 8 years. Due to budget cuts and my job role being slowly phased out, I decided to go back into classroom teaching to further prepare myself to one day becoming a principal. I felt I had learned a lot and gained valuable experience during my 8 years in the district office and wanted to utilize my acquired skills in the classroom. I joined the Ochoa faculty in the fall, just as the project was getting under way.

I distinctly remember receiving a dialogue schedule in my mailbox and going straight to the principal to ask if I had to attend. Her response was something like this: "Try it out. See what you think. If you don't like it or are not getting anything out of these sessions, you can bail out anytime. The sessions are not mandatory."

Now that I think back, I realize I was prepared to teach the very same way I had taught 15 years earlier, using textbooks, workbooks, and work sheets. I would make all the decisions as to what students were going to learn. I would make all the decisions as if it were my classroom, rather than our [the students' and my] classroom.

We'll learn in Chapter 2 that Marianne was not premature in preparing herself to become a principal.

CHRIS: I remember watching Paul [Heckman] present the possibility of school reinvention to the Ochoa staff. He was saying that we at the school would examine everything that we were doing—how we group children, who makes classroom decisions, what activities children should do, what we believe is essential for children to learn, how we evaluate that learning, and how parents, teachers, administrators, and the community should relate to one another. With Paul and the ECC Project staff, we would question everything, and rather than being asked to carry out someone else's plan, we teachers would be creating answers for ourselves.

I had long been aware of the incredible capabilities of children, and that schools rarely capitalize on the knowledge children bring with them to school, let alone take children's beliefs and desires into account as important decisions are made. I knew that parents do care about and want the best for their children, but that schools do not include parents as true partners in the education of their children.

I believed that schooling absolutely had to change, as the state of our nation and our world depends on citizens who can think for themselves and make sound decisions. I pictured learning extending beyond the walls of the school and into the community, where children would learn as they participate in work valued by the "outside world."

Earlier I had been part of Paul Heckman's Greater Tucson School-University Partnership. I admired his kindness, his respect for individuals, and the way he encouraged people to think. I wanted to be part of a support system that could help make our dreams for children a reality.

I very much hoped that the teachers would be excited and decide to participate and felt a wave of relief when Ochoa became a participant in the project. Yet, at the same time, I was well aware that although each person was making a commitment to "change," each had a different understanding of what that change could and would be. "At least," I thought to myself, "we're beginning the journey."

ANA: I was very impressed with what Paul Heckman said. He quoted statistics on the school dropout rate of Latino students and an even higher percentage rate for Native Americans. What was especially interesting to me was that he placed no blame on the students; he simply stated that what was being done in the name of education was not sufficient. That statement coincided with my thinking that every child can succeed, and in most cases the students don't fail, we fail.

Dr. Heckman proceeded to talk about "reinventing" and "rethinking" school. I asked myself: What do those terms mean? What came to mind was "out with the old and in with the new." He quoted studies that indicated the schoolwork done in low-income areas consisted of more drill- and skill-oriented activities and said that we were basing our education philosophy on the Industrial Era, when a high school education wasn't necessary to get worthwhile employment. During the presentation, I became excited because I was hearing a child advocate—a person speaking out for children in a way I had never heard before. So I just opened up my whole mind for that.

DELIA: Naive as it may sound, in the beginning, I didn't think this plan would take any extra effort, mentally or physically. I never thought I could get tired/exhausted in being creative about a plan I was truly interested in. I thought every new idea would just fall into place. I was naive.

CHRIS: I remember the very first day, when the principal came in to tell Sue and me that she'd just had a phone call from a district school administrator. She said something like: "We just got a grant for hundreds of thousands of dollars to create the school of the future."

There was truth in the matter of money being granted, but huge sums of money had been poured into educational reform all across the country, and researchers had learned that more money was not the single most important factor in educational reform. Somehow there never seems to be enough to do everything everyone envisions. The Ochoa teachers became aware of this too. Laura analyzed how people regard funding for schools in materialistic terms, rather than in changing or improving concepts, teaching practices, and structures.

LAURA: We now have an appreciation of how little hundreds of thousands of dollars can do, although it does pay for substitute teachers to allow us the opportunity to get together in the project's dialogue sessions. I think people have a material concept when they talk about spending money in education. They're thinking about books and computers and buildings and desks and that type of thing. They're not thinking in the context of building a school system internally in terms of teachers.

CHRIS: There really isn't enough money for all the things that were in my head when we began the project. The money is to help us rethink how traditionally we've been using money.

Ochoa faculty was almost euphoric in the beginning about the possibility of creating their own classroom curricula, straying from prescribed lesson plans or textbooks and developing their own individual teaching practices. However, as the project moved into its early months, these same teachers began to realize how much creativity, time, and effort the project was to take. It soon became obvious that true dedication in creating a "school of the future" would require a lot of work.

MARIANNE: In order for change to occur, it has to come from within, which means you have to want it, and my version of change may not be the same as my colleagues'. Also, changes will not occur overnight. Change is a continual development of ideas that takes time—time to implement your ideas and to see what works, what you want to keep, and what you want to toss out. It involves taking risks to do things differently and to plan or to exchange ideas with colleagues. One has to realize, too, that change involves a certain amount of ambivalence and ambiguity.

When the project began, you might say I was the new kid on the block, because I was coming back to a second-grade classroom after nearly a decade in the office of the school district. I wanted to participate in the project because I realized that things had to change. I didn't want to go back into teaching and the classroom in the very same traditional way; I knew there was more to teaching. I didn't want my students—or me—to become bored. I wanted to provide a challenging and stimulating environment in which children would be involved in their own learning, to be engaged as decision makers on topics they were interested in learning. Also, I wanted them to be responsible and investigate their own questions, using whatever resources necessary to answer their own questions. In short, I wanted my students to become critical thinkers and good problem solvers. All of this meant I had to change the way I had been taught to teach.

LINDA: I remember telling Paul [Heckman] how hard it was to work on all of the things we were working on at the same time—changing assessment, changing the work of kids, changing the work of teachers, changing the organization of how people worked together. The whole concept of school and community and parents and performances and all those things sometimes seemed overwhelming. I remember asking Paul: "Why are we doing this? Why are we doing all of this extra hard work?"

He said: "Well, if you don't know why we are doing it, maybe we shouldn't be doing it." When he said that, I remember thinking that not doing anything is even scarier. Everything that we've done is learning, which is far better than not taking any action about improving our kids' educations.

As time went by, teachers shared their beliefs, feelings, and practices. Simply by getting together and talking we had more information from which to work and make decisions. When we continue to add to our storehouse of information, change is the result.

Reflections

Competing feelings appear to loom large in what the teachers felt about participating in the project and creating the conditions to change. First, excitement and commitment ring loud and clear. Second, anxiety, tentativeness, and skepticism also are prevalent. These feelings compete, at times pulling individuals and group members toward our goals, at other times pushing them away from further examination and questioning and, hence, invention.

In addition, when a group of individuals invents the changes and puts them into practice, they are finding answers for themselves and are taking responsibility for what happens. In organizations characterized and governed by bureaucratic ideas, only those with authority carry much responsibility for specific and overall designs and actions in the system. Moreover, the assumption about teachers in such a bureaucratic organization is that they cannot and will not be responsible for their own actions, especially with regard to the design and implementation of what they understand education to be.

What then is unique in the ECC Project is that teachers were encouraged not only to invent but also to take responsibility for the design, the implementation, and the consequences of their inventions. They did not require anyone else to take care of them and shield them from the responsibility or the anxiety of such an endeavor.

Every inventor experiences highs and lows in figuring out or creating something. Inventors both believe and doubt that they can unravel the puzzle and make something new and unique. As they figure it out, however, they worry that what they have created is not quite "it"; but they go on. They have learned about the importance of skepticism and commitment.

These teachers, too, report the excitement and the anxiety associated with being responsible for this major charge to invent. Yet they opted to do it. The remainder of the book discusses what and how these responsibilities were undertaken and how emotions associated with such trust were addressed in the school and classrooms of Ochoa Elementary School.

2

Developing Dialogue Sessions

Dialogue sessions, which are attended once a week by the Ochoa teachers, the principal, and those teaching aides who want to attend, are now seen as a major key in creating conditions for school change. It is in dialogue where the culture of the school is explored, beliefs and ideas are freely exchanged, innovations are discussed, classroom successes and failures are celebrated or examined. During the early years of the project, emotions during the dialogue sessions ran especially high. Often feelings were hurt; yet the teachers endured and came to appreciate the peer support that resulted. Some teachers questioned being away from their classrooms for these hours; however, dialogue was soon seen as a necessary tool for change.

It was apparent that schoolwide change was neither probable nor possible at Ochoa under one existing condition that is prevalent in nearly all schools: Each teacher was more or less isolated in his or her classroom. Few knew what was going on in other classrooms; they seldom, if ever, talked to each other about their work, and there were few efforts among them that involved problem finding and problem solving. Consequently, the children did little collaborative problem finding and problem solving with their teachers or with other students.

It is my contention that teachers need the support of their peers if they are to pioneer new teaching practices. They need to talk, to exchange beliefs, and to discuss alternative ideas about their work. To do this, the teachers needed time together, so one of the first steps in ECC Project planning was to arrange for guest [substitute] teachers to take over classes at Ochoa during specified times that were set aside for teachers to attend what became the heart of the project: dialogue sessions.

To be effective, these dialogue sessions had to be intense and self-revealing. A guiding force was A. D. Gitlin's explanation of the difference in talk, conversation, and dialogue in *Harvard Educational Review* (1990):

- dialogue has importance and relevance to both parties, whereas talk may have no, some, or a lot of relevance to one but not the other party;
- dialogue seeks to promote understanding, whereas conversation tries to convince; and
- dialogue challenges taken-for-granted notions, whereas talk accepts them.

Although there was no design or agenda for the weekly sessions, that explanation of dialogue helped to define what the sessions were to be and distinguished them from traditional staff meetings or staff development sessions. But although I was uncertain if dialogue sessions were the right avenue to advance the project's goals for creating changes in teaching practices and school structures, my belief in the need for dialogue was reinforced at the initial presentation of the ECC Project to the Ochoa teachers.

LINDA: Dialogue sessions were first discussed when we met in the spring of 1990 with Paul Heckman to learn about the project. He asked us if we wanted to be part of a project to reinvent school and, if so, how were we going to do it? One of our first responses was: "We need time to talk with each other."

Dialogue, for some, took a great deal of courage, because to be effective, participants had to reveal a lot of themselves—to make public to each other their thoughts and beliefs about their teaching practices and to spell out their fears of change and dreams of the future.

These were not "meetings," in which someone presided and a prepared agenda was followed. No one was there to tell teachers what they should or should not do in their classrooms. Instead, I, in the beginning, and later, the project's research associates, were there as facilitators. We were both "outsiders" and "insiders." As outsiders, we asked questions and encouraged the teachers to pursue topics that they, themselves, introduced; as insiders, we felt free to express our beliefs and introduce ideas.

This public exchange in the dialogue sessions was a total departure from the past, when teachers worked independently of each other. They were now speaking about things that had been on their minds—perhaps as long as they had been teaching. The process and progress of dialogue are very evident on videotapes and audiotapes that document the dialogue sessions.

Often there were differences in ideas and intentions; emotions ran high and teachers sometimes felt offended. Stating what was in our minds and hearts often created anxieties and fear—fear of what others would think or feel. Would others be disappointed? Would others be hurt? What we had to address and acknowledge was the fact that "yes, others might be disappointed or hurt." But whose issue was that? And what responsibility did each of us have to be honest with our colleagues about what we wanted, knew, and felt? Moreover, can we live with conflict in schools? Early on, it became obvious that we often may disagree about ideas, feelings, and intentions and just have to live with the disagreement.

One session involved the flow of foot traffic through one of the offices. A staff member voiced the need to decrease traffic through her office in order to have fewer disruptions. Although this appeared on the surface to be a simple, single issue, the dialogue evolved into a multifaceted confrontation involving discussion of secondhand information and its content, the "pulling apart" of the staff, the workload in office and classrooms, and the lack of or need for equal treatment of all personnel. Because of goodwill and, I believe, good luck, modifications were made; we learned about working together and how to explore and try out ideas and practices.

Changing the beliefs of what is important in a school provoked some discomfort among those who participated in dialogue as well as those who didn't participate. The question was raised about teachers taking so much time away from their classrooms. What would happen to the children if teachers spent 20% of their work-week in dialogue sessions? This question had basis in the old idea that time on task has more importance than teachers inquiring and creating more powerful learning experiences. On the other hand, the thought of returning to the isolation and learned helplessness of former days did not have much appeal. Ultimately, ideas underlying the acceptance of the new structure of dialogue emerged: Teachers have intelligence, capacity, and responsibility for inventing new ideas and practices and examining and deciding the value of what they do. This focus altered the fundamental character of teachers' work from only being practical to also being theoretical—inquiring and inventing.

Disagreements would continue to occur, but all in all, dialogue provided a security for the risks being taken in making changes in the classrooms.

SUE: I sat through the early dialogue sessions, hopeful at first, but then getting more and more frustrated. Nobody seemed to know where we were supposed to go. We kept hashing and rehashing the same things, such as discipline, playground, and the like. I was so exhausted at the end of the early sessions that I would wish I had been teaching instead.

BECKY: I've always been a very quiet person, so in the beginning I didn't talk much during the sessions. I just kind of watched and listened. When the project staff asked me a question, I answered, but I was never one to volunteer an answer. It's different now; I feel more comfortable. I guess I developed trust. I felt I had some-thing that I could share, something of value, and if I didn't share it, well, others wouldn't know.

This whole thing has been good for me. I think the dialogue sessions have really brought me out.

ANA: Having this special time for teachers to just talk about issues pertaining to themselves and education was all so new to us. Although I was reluctant to say much in the beginning, I now have no problem sharing my thoughts with the whole group. I strongly feel that without the dialogue sessions there would be no change within us.

I remember the frustration we felt when we wanted answers to the "how to reinvent" questions and Paul didn't have the answers either. That was the impetus for us to put our heads together and try to work cohesively. There have been very uncomfortable and intense moments when we were dealing with personal relationships involving staff, but this has been necessary to clear the air and move forward. There were times when I didn't want to share the reinvention discoveries we had made, because I was witnessing skeptical looks and sometimes obvious inattention to what I was sharing. There is a risk factor when one is speaking out of the status quo lingo. Now, after 5 years, there is more questioning among us, rather than negative comments. We are still learning to speak with frankness and honesty without hurting one another's feelings. The important thing is, it's working.

LINDA: Before the project, I was pretty much by myself. The only time I interacted with colleagues was at lunchtime or if two classes were on the playground at the same time—or sometimes at staff meetings. I don't remember ever working with another teacher. We talked about working together—I remember talking to kindergarten teachers about having exchanges, but we never got around to it.

BECKY: Before participating in the project, I didn't think there was such a thing as interaction among colleagues. I knew people's names, but I didn't know anything about them. Actually it was very lonely. We were always in our classrooms and never really got to know anybody. Teaching is a lonely profession.

Dialogue sessions weren't battlefields, but they certainly provided a forum for airing differences. It was no time to be supersensitive, because someone might challenge whatever was said. While teachers learned more and more about the beliefs and practices of other teachers, they also found self-revelation in the sessions.

BECKY: Sometimes in the dialogue sessions, I felt I was being attacked by the facilitator. If I said something, he would press on to find out why I felt a certain way, why I believed what I said to be true. I know now why he would pursue a point, but it took a lot of dialogue sessions for that not to bother me. Even now I don't know that it doesn't bother me, but I can handle it now.

LINDA: Dialogue sessions were very emotional sometimes. And sometimes they were heated, and I felt attacked. I used to think that everyone should be doing what I was doing in the classroom; it worked for me, so why doesn't everybody try it? I didn't realize that some people are ready to take on the kind of challenge the project offered, and others are not. It really took me about a year to accept that people are where they are in life, and I shouldn't worry about that. I just have to let them be there. I remember feeling that people who weren't really trying to change their teaching practices—or weren't doing something toward change— were kind of holding back the rest of us.

Then in one dialogue session we talked about children being ready for different things and that, ideally, we should allow each child to develop at his or her own pace. It occurred to me that if we allow for every child's individuality, then we should offer the same to teachers. Now I can say that I do accept, but don't completely understand, why some people might not want to engage in a project such as this. However, at that time I also began to realize just how much work—hard work—this project requires.

BECKY: There was a lot of conflict in some dialogue sessions, and we walked out with knots in our stomachs. Those caused tension for me. I wanted to crawl out of—I don't know how many—meetings, because I don't like to argue. But we had to learn how to handle conflicts and move on. We had plenty of disagreements, especially during the third year, and although the conflict wasn't good, bringing conflicts into the open and coming to resolutions of them was good.

As prescribed textbooks, worksheets, and memorization processes became a thing of the past, self-doubt would sometimes emerge.

DELIA: I found myself becoming alienated from teachers who had been my friends as I became more verbal about the philosophical changes I was experiencing. Substitute teachers, who take over on the days of dialogue sessions, are a concern to me, whether they're good teachers or not so good. I overheard one in the personnel office saying she could not help my students because there were no alphabet letters pinned up in my classroom. Another explained that she found it hard to work with the children because there were no number charts in my room. One substitute among those I admired said she wasn't sure of the quality of learning that was going on in my classroom.

My concern is that my reputation is at risk in doing all of these wonderful things. I understand and believe in what I'm doing. My teammates understand and believe in me, as do my students, but in the meantime I hear all of these adverse comments. I keep thinking that a few of us are just "before our time."

LAURA: I think dialogue really began to make an impact during the second year of the project. Before, I wasn't sure how my work in the classroom was being perceived. I felt I was treading madly in deep water, because I was doing so many different things, and I didn't know how to evaluate what I was doing. There was no basis for assessment.

The weekly dialogue sessions became my support system. We could go into those sessions and cry, complain, celebrate and lean on people who would help hold us up. That interaction with my colleagues became an integral part of my week and enabled me to continue the reinvention process in the classroom.

BECKY: Dialogue provided support in that I would hear other people saying they did this or tried that, and it would encourage me to break whatever I was doing and try something else. It was uncomfortable at first, but it got to be a little more comfortable.

SUE: As time went by, the value of dialogue became more apparent. I'm still not sure about many concepts that were discussed and put into practice, but these sessions put all of us together, and I began to know more about the primary people and actually feel that all parts of the school were working together.

MARIANNE: At the beginning of the project, I was more an observer than an active participant. I needed to feel myself within the group, but I hadn't developed the confidence or the trust among the faculty or staff. Then later I started taking risks and speaking out. There were some sessions that you just didn't want to be a part of because they were heated discussions about your philosophy and beliefs. There were some dialogues where people felt they were being attacked over a statement or comment or misinterpretation. Some dialogue sessions had to do with searching deep inside and it sometimes took guts to say "I disagree . . . " or "That's not true."

I know now that dialogue sessions are important. They provide a type of communication that continues throughout the week with students, within your team, and with other faculty members. Getting together weekly encouraged me to make some changes in my classroom and to exchange ideas and interact with my colleagues. Changes don't occur in leaps and bounds, so I was taking one step at a time and then reflecting on those changes. It also seems to me that disagreement and conflict among the faculty are necessary in order for change to occur. This can lead to lots of frustrations; however, I don't feel I could have gotten to the point where I am in reinvention without the dialogue process.

DELIA: Dialogue sessions serve many different purposes. It is a time for me to test the waters. There always are a lot of questions, such as "How did you do" certain things or "How much time did you spend on" something. I kept looking for the teachers' consensus to change, and I confused their questions with their general agreement. In one instance, I went ahead with Chris and initiated a study unit about pumpkins [see Chapter 6, this volume]. We were enthusiastic about the pumpkin study and presented our findings at a dialogue session. I found the teachers to be intrigued by the type of study, but I felt that most of them weren't convinced it was or could possibly be academic. I heard comments such as, "It's just a passing fad."

Upon reflection, Chris and I feel the pumpkin unit taught our first-graders far more than any science book we've ever used during our years of traditional teaching.

CHRIS: It seems to me that in the beginning dialogue was critical in order to get common language and common thought throughout the school. Although no one was required to go, the more who went, the better. But during the third year, I began wondering if some people wouldn't do better within a smaller group. One teacher did not find a comfort level in the dialogue sessions [with between 18 and 22 participants], and I kept wondering if, over time, we would identify this situation and each teacher could be in a setting that is comfortable for him or her.

LAURA: Most people seemed to agree that a dialogue group with all of the teachers and many of the aides was too large. It was unwieldy, and people's contributions were fewer. I think there's a need to redesign the system in terms of numbers of people. Comfort levels seem to diminish as the number of people increases.

During the third year, I had a real desire to get back to my former dialogue group, which had only 10 or 12 people in it [the faculty and aides were divided into two dialogue groups]. It was a real cross-section, but there was a cohesiveness that was definitely missing in a larger group. I thought my former group was the one that was really participating in this project, and its commitment to the project was what built the whole support process for me.

CHRIS: An interesting tension that exists in dialogue is the need to have diverse opinions to challenge people and make them think. And yet, dialogue among people who continually and fundamentally disagree can stop the group from being the support system it needs to be.

SUE: Five years ago, when the project began, I was a Title 1 teacher, working with small groups of students. Dialogue on Fridays had been a time to interact with all teachers, not just those whose students I saw. During the third and fourth years, I was a resource teacher, spending half my time with one team and the other half with different teachers and projects.

In the fifth year my role changed again, and I became a full-time intermediate [fourth- and fifth-grade] classroom teacher/researcher, involved in a small-class-size model. I have responsibilities for my own group of children and, at the same time, am involved in a team with Laura and another teacher, exploring different ways of working with children. For the first time, I feel the concern teachers have expressed about being away from their students for extended periods of time. I'm protective of my time in the classroom, and yet, dialogue remains critical if we are to make changes.

My first experience with a guest teacher on dialogue day had its ups and downs. Initially, the class and I were excited because our guest teacher came with a background in dance and drama—two areas I both loved and needed help exploring. She worked really hard with the students, even writing a play for them, based on "Damn Yankees." But there were management problems with the students, which required me to leave the dialogue session and return to the classroom most afternoons, thereby losing time with my teammates. This, combined with time each of us has missed for personal reasons, made our planning sessions nearly nonexistent.

Common dialogue time is essential to further the exchange of ideas; however, when it takes precedence over the individual needs of participants, something is wrong. I found this problem when my teammates and I began concentrating on the subject of student assessment. My team felt it imperative that we spend time together on the assessment process. Laura and I wanted to use our dialogue time to talk, to recreate, modify, and make adjustments in our assessment work, yet we were expected in dialogue sessions. I understand the need to share with the total group and keep communication open, but I feel that dialogue time needs to be flexible enough to change with the changing needs of its participants.

Reflections

This chapter has focused on what the teachers, principal, and I call dialogues, which, during the fifth year, happen on a weekly basis for an entire school day at Ochoa. Guest teachers are provided to allow all of the participants to be together and exchange ideas. The sessions appear to be contributing to changes in the classrooms and lives of the teachers and, as we will see later, in the children who attend Ochoa.

Dialogue schedules have changed each year. During the first year, teachers met in two groups on the same day of the week. The teachers were brought into the groups in a random fashion, with only a consideration to have different grade-level teachers in each group. As the first year of the project drew to an end, both groups recommended consolidation of the two groups; common issues were being addressed and several efforts to try out new practices and structures were under way by different members of each group. Perhaps, if dialogue happened with the groups combined, more connections could be encouraged among members of the school community.

During the last half of the second year, teachers wanted another change and asked for permission to release students early one day a week and make up the instructional time by beginning school earlier and ending it later on other days of the week. District administrators approved the proposal, and teachers arranged to begin dialogue at 1 p.m. and end at 3 p.m. on the early release day. However, because of the negotiated teachers' agreement, teachers could leave the dialogue at 2:30 p.m., which some of them often did. At an early point in the fall of that year, I realized that the intensity of the dialogues had diminished; teachers and teaching assistants were meeting with the principal and project staff for only 90 minutes. Conversation and talk were replacing true dialogue.

Meanwhile, teachers were trying out several new structures and classroom activities that had grown out of the first year's dialogues. Some were combining multiage classes, and some had gone beyond that, mixing Spanish-dominant and English-dominant multiage students. Perhaps they had gone too far too fast; teachers began expressing frustrations with the new groupings they had undertaken in their classrooms, and they were finding it difficult to figure out what the curriculum and classroom activities should be under these more heterogeneous circumstances.

On several occasions, the principal, Elsa Padilla, and I discussed the fact that several teachers had suggested to her that these new, problematic arrangements had really been foisted upon the school by the two of us. We were surprised; we had the sense that group members had made these decisions—with our support, of course, and videotapes of earlier dialogues showed that participants had agreed among themselves to make these changes. However, we began to understand what happens to good people when change is under way. More important, we agreed that we were witnessing what happens when insufficient time is allotted for dialogue.

By November, I was very worried and, after talking with Elsa, I invited anyone who was interested to participate in a 3-day dialogue retreat; guest teachers were engaged for the teachers who accepted. By the end of the first day of the retreat, much had been aired, new questions and issues were surfacing, and new ideas were being explored. By the end of the third day, it was agreed that all-day dialogue sessions would be held one day a week for those who wanted that kind of intensity. For those who didn't want the all-day experience, there was agreement that no decisions would be made that would affect nonparticipants, and issues that might have an impact others would be brought to a full staff meeting. For the rest of the year, dialogue involved a smaller number of individuals than it had in the fall; however, this group developed tightly shared ideas and commitments to one another, and all-day dialogue sessions once a week became the norm.

Another change occurred late in the second year when the project's funding partners agreed to expand the project to a second elementary school. The expansion meant that I could no longer facilitate all dialogue sessions, and Viki Montera, the project coordinator who had worked as a research associate for the first 2 years at Ochoa, began facilitating dialogues at the additional school and working with Chris Confer, a Title 1 resource teacher and one of the authors of this book, who agreed to lead the dialogue sessions at Ochoa. I would work closely with Chris and Viki and sometimes facilitate the meetings, but if this work was to one day lead to systemic change, I had to devote time to coordinating many diverse aspects of the

project. Also, it was important to determine the dialogue
conditions that contribute to the promotion of change—
beyond my personal experience as a facilitator. It was also
necessary to determine if facilitators can be developed to
do what I did.

In the third year, Ochoa teachers were to experience
another unexpected change: Elsa Padilla developed serious back problems and took a leave of absence. It was an
unsettling event; as principal, she had provided the permission and leadership for accomplishing much of what
transpired during the first 2 ½ years. Fortunately, everything did not come to an abrupt stop, thanks to Marianne
Chavez, who had administrative interest and experience
and, as the reader may remember from Chapter 1, had
returned to Ochoa and had aspirations to one day become
a school principal. With Marianne serving as acting principal and with the cooperation of Chris as dialogue facilitator and the competence and support of the entire Ochoa
faculty and staff, the project continued to move forward.

Although each of these events and changes brought
about lengthy discussions and anxieties, agreements
were reached and alterations were made with relative
ease. I believe that can be partially attributed to the lack
of a specific design for dialogue sessions. Lacking a specific design, however, does not suggest that ideas did not
guide the development of the dialogues and other project
work. Quite the contrary.

The development of dialogues at the school exemplifies
one attempt to use a new set of ideas. The establishment
of time for teachers to discuss their practices and the
ideas underlying them, as well as to explore and create
new ideas and practices, signaled a new significance of
teachers' thoughts and actions.

As their comments reveal, most teachers who participated in the dialogues came to value this time for various
reasons. For some, dialogue reduced the isolation and
loneliness of teaching so long characteristic of schools.
Others talked about the support that their colleagues
gave them. They also spoke of dialogue encouraging new
ideas and practices that came from these weekly meet-

ings. However, the emotional side cannot be overlooked; some of the sessions produced headaches, anxiety, and temporary unhappiness. Perhaps those represent the price to be paid for change.

As seems to be characteristic in schools, conflict is avoided and not seen as positive at Ochoa. In this chapter, teachers have addressed and examined the norm that "conflict is scary and to be avoided." It is my hope that teachers and teams of teachers in the future will encourage members to be different, to ask questions that may engender conflict, and that by encouraging and addressing different views and ideas, conflict will be seen as positive—as providing strength to teams and the education of children.

Irrespective of the differences that surely exist among individuals and groups of adults, I hope that unconditional acceptance—what psychotherapist Carl Rogers calls "unconditional positive regard"—will prevail in dialogue sessions, teaming, and all other project activities. Not only does unconditional regard have importance in productive endeavors, it also has certain reciprocal benefits for everyone; for instance, if I have unconditional regard for my colleagues—no matter what their beliefs may be—a greater likelihood exists that my colleagues will have that same regard for me. Hence, in team experiences and in conversations across teams, I can be more expressive of who I am, what I believe, and what I understand. Even though differences will surely exist and conflicts will arise, such variation will only mean that there are differences, not that people are bad because they see the world in different ways.

Such regard and the capacity to live with differences will forward the inquiry that the project has advocated as essential in reinventing education. As individuals more and more examine and express what they know and understand, the more inquiry will happen and thus more reinvention will take place. Unconditional regard may be essential for individuals to really say what they know and understand, especially with the foreknowledge that differences in these areas are inevitable and terrible things will not happen when differences are expressed. Meetings of individuals trying to create something often have starts and stops, meanderings, and revisiting of particular ideas and strategies. Conflicts arise, but in many cases the resolution of conflict often yields the best results.

Reference

Gitlin, A. D. (1990, November). Educative research, voice, and school change. *Harvard Educational Review,* pp. 447-448.

3

Supporting Colleagues
Through Team Teaching

As teachers became more knowledgeable about their own beliefs and the ideas and beliefs of others on the faculty, they began talking about various school structures, such as language tracking and graded classrooms. The logical accommodation for changing some of the traditional school structures seemed to lie in teachers' collaborating as teammates. Although the concept of team teaching was not new, at Ochoa the work cut out for the teaching teams was different from many efforts of the past, and selecting the right partner with whom to undertake this new work was a critical issue.

Although the dialogue sessions broke down some of the barriers of teacher isolation at Ochoa, the general structure of the school remained virtually the same. But shortly thereafter, multilingual and multiage grouping of students became a focus, and the idea of teams of teachers who were responsible for more than one classroom was discussed as a viable alternative to the isolation in the "egg crate" school. They were not considering departmentalization, in

which a class is taught one subject by one teacher and another
subject by another teacher and so on. Nor were they considering a
system in which all teachers teach all of the students. What evolved
were teams of two and sometimes three teachers who had responsibility for all the learning of two or three classes. In most cases the
mix of classes spans at least 2 years or grades. For example,
Marianne's second-grade and Becky's third-grade classes are mixed.
The intermediate mix was of fourth, fifth, and sixth grades, until the
fifth year of the project, when sixth grade became part of the middle
school rather than of the elementary school. In the case of Ana and
Delia, each teaches first grade, and they mix the two classes of
6-year-olds.

One may immediately ask, what's new about team teaching?
Didn't elementary schools try out team teaching in the sixties? Aren't
you just recreating the wheel rather than inventing a new structure
and set of practices?

Elementary schools in the sixties did try out an innovation called
team teaching; however, the team teaching of the sixties did not have
undergirding it the same set of new ideas that were developing at
Ochoa. There may have been some overlap of ideas in the sixties, but
six concepts undergird the efforts at Ochoa as team teaching continue to develop and be refined:

1. Each team comprises a small decentralized unit of the school
   whose members create a program for a group of students with
   whom these teachers work together for at least 2, and sometimes 3, years.
2. Each team has the responsibility to create unique classroom
   structures, schedules, curriculum, and assessment for their
   students and themselves, while they also connect these practices to the ideas and activities of other teams.
3. Each team seeks connections and relationships to each student and his or her family. By developing these connections
   over several years, deeper relationships can be established
   and further promote student learning and achievement.
4. Each team becomes another setting for engaging in inquiry,
   invention, and examination on dialogue day as well as other
   days of the week.
5. Each team creates criteria for and ways of assessing the
   worth of what children know and the quality of the student

work, structures, and practices of each team. These criteria and ways of assessing connect to the criteria and assessment practices of other teams.

6. The ideas or elements of the school that each team holds in common with other teams are formed from what each team uniquely does, and these ideas and actions merge to form the total character and culture of the school.

As teachers discuss teaming in this chapter, their concepts of teaming are reflected in the issues and enthusiasm or concerns expressed as they developed and continue to expand team teaching at Ochoa. Although there was an outward expression of enthusiasm for team teaching in the beginning, some teachers revealed, at a later time, the trepidation they had felt about various aspects of it. As with anything that involves a number of people, personalities were something to be considered, and this became very apparent when the teachers decided to teach in teams. One teacher was extremely fearful that she would be teamed in the classroom with a teacher whose methods and practices differed from hers. The results of that pairing will never be known, because the teacher bonded with another teacher in a good relationship.

It was made clear by the principal Elsa Padilla as well as the ECC Project staff that teachers were not obligated to team teach. It was a personal option, and there was no prescribed way of teaming. Thoughts about teaming were mixed. Some teachers seemed to dread the possibility of team teaching, others looked forward to trying it. One teacher said: "I honestly don't want to work alone." But finding and working with a teammate can pose problems.

LAURA: I feel that there are some people I can't work with, because we may be coming from different philosophies or methods or ideas or something.

CHRIS: All of us [teachers] are in different places, asking different questions and pursuing different alternatives.

LAURA: About 20 years before the project began I had a team teaching experience that was a disaster. I had no choice of teammates, and the person I was teaching with imposed his philosophy and methodology on all aspects of our teaching. Therefore,

I was extremely apprehensive when team teaching was mentioned as part of the project. But by the time we initiated it, we had been involved in dialogue for several months and I was comfortable with my choice of partners. The difference was, in this case, we teachers were the ones who initiated the partnerships.

Team teaching among this group of teachers was generally looked upon favorably, but after a few weeks Sue expressed some misgivings:

SUE: At first, I didn't like the idea of team teaching, but more and more I see that it benefits my students as well as myself.

Avoiding or getting out of a mismatch caused tension for some teachers. They found saying, "I don't want to work with you," to be impossible or, at the very least, a hardship. Laura said in one case she just "flat out said it."

LAURA: I felt the need to do it. It's gotten to the point now where so much of this [alternative teaching] is time-consuming and hard work. I know that I can't do it by myself, and if I'm not sure that the other teacher is willing to contribute equally, I won't do it.

I work well with Delia, Sue, Lina Valdez, and some other teachers, because I know what my limits are, and I can express that to them and they will accept it—and vice versa. And I also know that when we're pursuing something, each of us is working hard at what we're doing. Sometimes we're working hard from different perspectives, but we're working equally hard at it.

It has something to do with learning your own boundaries. The big questions are "Where do we get the time?" and "How do we work through all these things with the people we are committed to working with?" There has to be a boundary; otherwise, I don't think I would have the strength to continue.

And there are personality differences. I think we need to be aware and acknowledge that there are those teachers we don't enjoy working with. In the long run, there is a certain amount of joy that goes with what we're doing—watching our progress, evaluating results, sharing some of the little things with each other. There's a joy in that, and that joy is what keeps us going, because, all in all, it's tough work. And if you don't enjoy being with someone, it's very, very taxing.

A certain built-in trust is required when teaming with another teacher. It involves revealing a lot of one's self to another—baring one's knowledge, skills, creativity, and inventiveness.

DELIA: Early on, I was afraid my teammate would criticize my spontaneity, my curiosity, my informality, my taking risks (and sometimes falling flat on my face). I felt I had been an excellent traditional teacher, but wondered if that reputation would vanish if this other professional teacher viewed what I am doing as ineffective, unorganized, and unprofessional. In my heart I just wanted to let go, to actually enjoy teaching and be effective at the same time. I wanted to know and respect students as people and for them to feel the same about me. I wanted students to see that I, too, was curious about life and the earth and that we could learn together. Did my teammate really have the same ideas about teaching, or would she report me as unprofessional?

Compatibility of personalities and similarity of good intentions were factors in establishing a good team of teachers; however, Delia found there were even more important factors. She describes the beginning of the third year of the project:

DELIA: At the end of the second year of the ECC Project I was determined to go on with it. Two other first-grade teachers and I formed a team and worked all summer formulating a program of priorities and values. We agreed that we wanted to make changes, but there were things and certain practices we felt we must retain. We said such things as "I want to change things, but I don't want the furniture [desks] moved in the classroom," or "I want to make changes, but I don't want to give up work sheets" (with such excuses as "the kids love them"). So we made a list of things or conditions we felt we must have—things we felt should be retained as other things were changed. We called this our "must have" list.

Then—almost suddenly—it was the start of another school year—always a hectic time. We hardly were aware the first few weeks that our plans of the summer fell by the wayside. Not only had we forgotten about our new ideas and list of "must haves," but we had also unconsciously gone back to our old routines and teaching practices.

We regrouped to try to figure out what had happened and decided we had simply taken the easy way out during a time of stress. We had gravitated back to the familiar, and therefore comfortable, ways of working. It had been so easy to go back to the customary, and yet it was not as comfortable as in years past. The old teaching practices were not as "right" and "wise" as in prior years; work with the project had changed me and subconsciously changed what I believed to be right.

My team met with the support team from the project to discuss how our summer plans had failed and we discovered that communication among our team members had not been as incisive as it should have been. We thought we had the same dreams; we thought we heard the same things coming from each other, but, in fact, we were not really listening to each other's messages. All three of us wanted to move ahead, be progressive, and be innovative, but our definitions of progressive and innovative were different. In fact, the way each of us wanted to move ahead was not conducive to our teaming. We were good friends and meant well, but teaming has nothing to do with well meaning or friendships. We needed a similar philosophy of teaching and to be at the same level of risk taking.

I concluded that teammates need to embrace the same theoretical framework with similar ideas about who children are and what knowledge they bring from their homes and cultures. A teammate of mine must believe that children are intelligent, resourceful, and capable beings with diverse abilities, skills, and talents, as well as emotional, intellectual, physical, and spiritual needs. There also must be concurrence that education as we know it today is ineffective and limiting for some students and that language diversity is an asset, not a liability.

As far as the "must have" list was concerned, we learned that there are things we must give up—past conditions must be changed if we are to reinvent education. It might have been more helpful if we had made a list of "must give ups." In the back of my mind was the question: Once I give "something" up, what will I replace that something with, and why?

SUE: Earlier, when I was working only with grades 3 through 6, I rarely saw the primary teachers. As a Title 1 teacher, I was doing computer instruction with at-risk students who were pulled from their regular classrooms, and I interacted with other teachers primarily about individual children's progress, or lack of it, but very little else.

An exception was Laura, because we shared a love of music and drama. About 10 years ago we began staging and producing a series of costumed and choreographed musicals with the students. I worked with a few other teachers in similar ways, but being a team for a project with an immediate common conclusion was different from teaming on a more permanent basis.

MARIANNE: I was very hesitant to ask anyone to team. I really liked the neat activities Becky was doing in her class but didn't know how to approach her. I guess I was sure I wanted to team with her but didn't know whether she wanted to team with me. About that time Elsa, our principal, routed a sheet to the teachers asking such questions as: "What grade would you like to teach?" "Would you like to team teach?" "If so, with whom?" It was then that I learned Becky and I had mutual feelings about teaching, so we decided to become a team. I was the bilingual second-grade teacher, and Becky, although bilingual, was the monolingual-English third-grade teacher.

I remember that we were feeling very frustrated at first, not knowing what to do or how to do it. Here we were, with two different grade levels and a mix of Spanish-dominant and English-dominant students, not knowing which direction to turn.

We thought about asking Elsa, the principal, if we could keep the team concept but go back to teaching one class in English and the other in Spanish, but instead we decided to give the mixed classes a try. After all, if we didn't try it, we would never know. We're now into our third year as a team, simultaneously teaching a class of 7- and 8-year-olds in both English and Spanish.

BECKY: Team teaching eliminated the loneliness of teaching, and that was something I had always wanted. My teammate, Marianne, and I did a lot of things together. Each of us had 30 students, and at one point we tried to combine the two classes

during the entire day. We found that was too chaotic, especially
because I had eight boys with behavior problems. It was just too
difficult for a long period, so, in the beginning, we combined the
classes only during fun periods, such as phys. ed., music, or
sometimes with an art project. We later extended the time the
classes had together.

I think both classes understood that we, the teachers, were
together, and it didn't matter that Gerardo was in Marianne's
class or Edgar was in mine. The way the kids saw it, they were
in both classes. I think the reason the children understood that
is because first thing in the morning, just after taking attendance and other morning tasks, we made our exchange of students. The English-dominant students would come to me, and
my Spanish-dominant students would go to her. Both of us, of
course, are bilingual. Then both classes would have recess at the
same time, so there wasn't the feeling of "belonging" to either
teacher.

Marianne and I handled situations in very much the same
way, and we were very good about letting each other know about
what happened in our classrooms. For instance, one of us would
say to the other that a student was having a bad morning and
could use some special attention—or a student did something
especially well and could use some praise or recognition. The kids
knew that they couldn't get away with stuff; they knew we talked
a lot and they felt there was consistency as far as consequences
were concerned. The kids really picked up on that and the classes
became a big ol' happy family.

LINDA: When my teammate and I combined our classes, I felt very
supported. I felt as if we were good role models for our kids when
we talked things out in front of them. We'd talk about what we
wanted to do next, and the children felt very stable that we were
both together and we both knew what was going on. They knew
we supported each other.

Becky and Linda agree that teachers don't have to be friends to
work well together as a team. Although Linda and her teammate
were friends before they began working together, Becky and Marianne became friends as a result of working together.

LINDA: Even though we were friends, we didn't know that we both would handle problems the same way before we started teaching together. Our philosophies were the same, and that's an important thing in teaming.

BECKY: I believe flexibility is more important than being friends. I am not so set on how to do something that I will never accept another way. I'm open to criticism and I'm open to change. Because I'm doing something one way doesn't mean I'm going to do it the same way for the next 20 years. I think it's important to be willing to listen to your partner. One of us would say we were going to do something, and the other would say, "Okay, I'll do it too." It would take us a very short time to act, because we were both agreeable and flexible.

When a compatible teammate moves to another school or leaves for other reasons, a tremendous loss can be felt. It's a breakdown in the remaining teacher's support system—a new beginning with new anxieties.

LINDA: I was teaching the monolingual [English-dominant] fourth-grade class, and the teaching position in the bilingual [Spanish-dominant] fourth-grade class became vacant. Earlier, I had become friends with Susanna Durón when she was teaching first grade at our school, and we had talked a lot about our beliefs about language and curriculum. We both questioned the monolingual-bilingual track system and talked about how much fun it would be to work together. She applied for the fourth-grade bilingual teaching position and got the job. We worked well together for 2 years, chipping away at the language wall between students. We had the ideal partnership.

Then Susanna got married and moved to Alaska. Although I was happy for her, I felt lost. I didn't realize just how much I would miss her until the start of the next school year. I remember I kept asking myself how that kind of teaching partnership could be duplicated.

Although the beliefs of my new teammate are similar to mine and we work well together in some areas, that earlier partnership was unique. I feel it will never be duplicated, even if we were to teach together again. I've resolved that in my mind and have learned just to appreciate the fact that I had that experience.

Now, in my second year with my new teammate, our relationship is growing. We're talking more and doing more things together. When she came into the project, she had not had the previous 2 years of dialogue I had experienced, nor had she tried new things in the classroom as project teachers were permitted to do. We do have common beliefs about children, how they learn, how to communicate with them positively, and how they acquire knowledge. I'm optimistic about our classes and our partnership.

There are as many team teaching possibilities as there are people. The mystery is how people can work together, but not necessarily look at things the same. Teaming is as unique as the people involved.

In the third year of the project, when Elsa went on medical leave from her position as principal, Becky's teammate, Marianne, left her classroom to become the acting principal, thus dissolving their team relationship.

BECKY: In the beginning I was very hesitant about teaming, but I made the decision to team with Marianne, and I couldn't have chosen a better partner. We hit it off immediately. Both of us have a good sense of humor and great flexibility, which added fun to our day. Then in the middle of the project's third year, my hopes for the team effort were shattered when Marianne became acting principal. It was supposed to be a temporary change, but it lasted through the end of the school year. Everything changed for me.

My teammate during that semester was a new teacher who, understandably, needed a period of orientation in the teaching field. I felt she needed her space, so during that year, team teaching ended for me after the first semester.

The greatest fear I had was going back into isolation. The good experience of teaming had convinced me that teaching in isolation is definitely not a good thing for me.

At the start of the fourth year of the project, Elsa returned as principal, and Marianne resumed teaching as a team with Becky.

MARIANNE: We both feel comfortable and have learned quite a bit from each other and from the students. Becky and I seem to have the same beliefs; we're constantly bouncing ideas off of each other. We go through the same emotions: happy and excited or sad and feeling down. And when one of us is discouraged or down, each of us does a good job of lifting the other. Team teaching is so much better than working in isolation as we did in the past.

A change of partners wasn't always an upsetting event. In fact, some teachers felt they benefited by working with different teammates.

LAURA: During the first 3 years in the project, I had the opportunity to develop and experience several types of team teaching partnerships. Teammate changes (caused by choice or through transfer) have been very positive for me. I've enriched and expanded my learning through their strengths. Each experience is a new challenge, and although I don't feel all of my/our goals can be accomplished during a partnership, I know I achieve many more goals than I would teaching alone. Also, I think I'm able to contribute more to my current and future teammates because of my previous partners and experiences.

When team teaching was initiated, only primary grades were combined, and I was teaching a monolingual (English) fifth-grade class. I was one of the teachers who advocated extending multiage/grade grouping to include intermediate students. I teamed with a third-grade bilingual teacher and a sixth-grade bilingual teacher. The idea of integrating the intermediate grades was initiated to provide data and information about multiage, bilingual grouping for our dialogue group. Actually, this effort was so successful that it provided the impetus for combining all of the intermediate classes.

Every year I become more enthusiastic about team teaching. Aside from experience gained in working with other teachers, it provides an opportunity to know and work with a larger number of students, and it's altered my perception of many students and their perceptions of me. Students with whom I'd only had brief, sometimes negative, encounters in the hallways have become buddies who come to my classroom after school just to talk or to offer their help. I can't imagine working alone and returning to the isolation of single-grade-level classes.

ANA: For the first 3 years, I participated in the project as a Title 1
    bilingual resource teacher and reading recovery teacher, but as
    time went by I realized I would like to have my own classroom.
    I could see some of the things that were happening in the
    classrooms and was inspired. I wanted to try some of my own
    ideas, so I asked to go back to classroom teaching.

    Six-year-olds are the children I love to work with, and my
    request to teach that age group was granted. Then I approached
    Delia about being my teammate. I had been especially interested
    in some of the things she was doing in her class; she seemed to
    believe that anything is possible. So in 1993 our exciting adven-
    ture began as a first-grade bilingual team.

    Delia's strong belief that anything is possible was especially
    evident at the beginning of the 1994 school year, when we had
    the idea of creating a music program for our first-graders.

    We questioned the district's and school's rationale of wait-
    ing to offer instructions on musical instruments until a student
    reaches the fourth- or fifth-grade level. (Even at that level, there
    is no formalized fine arts program except for band and orchestra.)

    We felt it appropriate to implement the new program through
    the use of instruments and music that are familiar to the stu-
    dents' home environment, which in most cases meant *mariachi,*
    the music of Mexican street bands comprised of guitarists, vio-
    linists, and trumpeters. Some children in our classes could al-
    ready play the guitar to some degree, and many of the parents
    were quite adept at it.

    To carry out our mission of initiating the music program, we
    needed permission and funds. That was when Delia kept saying,
    "We can do it." So, together we wrote a proposal to the Arizona
    Commission of Arts to create a *mariachi* music program for our
    first-graders. Being involved in restructuring and reinventing
    our teaching practices through the ECC Project had given us
    more confidence to pursue what we believed was right for our
    students. Although we had missed the deadline for the proposal
    (which we were not aware of at the time), we didn't accept the
    word "no" gracefully. Because Elsa, our principal, was ill during
    this time, we walked the proposal through Elaine Rice, assistant
    superintendent in our school district. There were a few stum-
    bling blocks, but Delia was right: We could do it; our proposal
    was accepted, and Delia and I as a team felt a great bonding.

DELIA: A teammate provides a lot of emotional security in trying new ideas, such as those we try in the ECC Project. Sometimes I fear that at the end of the project there will have been no systemic changes in the school district's regulations, and I will lose the teammate who has supported my dreams and encouraged my risk taking. And I also fear having a new principal with a traditional philosophy.

Reflections

By the end of the third year, team teaching had become a constant with many of the teachers at Ochoa. Three teachers had teamed to teach three first-grade classes; two teachers had teamed to teach the combined second- and third-graders, and six teachers were teaming in a combination of fourth-, fifth-, and sixth-grade classes. Within that basic teaming practice, there were teams within teams. For example, Laura, Sue, Lina Valdez, and Linda were teamed in the Spanish-English production of an original play script, based on the story of "Snow White." Isolation for these teachers was a thing of the past; they knew each other, spent time with each other, attended workshops together, discussed students' progress and achievement, or lack of it. Students had grown accustomed to having more than one teacher and were deriving benefit from a greater variety of teacher expertise and creativity.

By mid-term of the fourth year of the project, one could observe that virtually all of the participating teachers were pleased with team teaching and appreciated the opportunity to share their knowledge and skills with their peers and to work collaboratively.

A message that has come through the voices of teachers in this chapter is the importance of working or teaming with colleagues who have similar interests, ideas/philosophies, and teaching methods. An explanation given in this chapter for the apparent success of most teaming efforts is that differences among team members were reduced by finding like-minded colleagues. At this point in the development of the project, this principle of homogeneity seems to be effective and contributing to the reinvention of organizational structures within the school.

Some of the early arguments made in support of team teaching in the sixties also highlighted the principle of homogeneity as a crucial dimension for successful teams. Moreover, the sorting of children according to their differences has been a major activity and focus in most schools. For example, same-age classes have prevailed in the belief that having students of a similar age reduces variability among the students and makes teacher and student work more effective.

Instead of separating students or adults to find commonality I had hoped that within the project the teachers, principals, parents, and project staff might develop capacities to see differences and heterogeneity as positive, productive, and advantageous for all. Furthermore, I hoped that through the interaction of very diverse individuals, new ways to build commonness would emerge and that diversity would be revealed as a strength.

Obviously, at this point in the development of the project, such a belief is not fully accepted; however, perhaps as our work continues, teams will form because of the diverse strengths and interests of individuals in a school. If such a principle advances in the school, a broad range of interests, knowledge, and skills among students and teachers could further enhance individual development and common understandings about the world.

Benefits and problems of combining multilingual classes and multiage/grade classes will be discussed in the following two chapters and will provide further evidence of the advantages and disadvantages of team teaching.

4

Getting Off Track

For two decades students at Ochoa had been divided into two languages tracks, often referred to as language "strands," and despite all efforts, literacy rates were low in both English- and Spanish-dominant classes. Also, more and more students came to think of their language group as an entity, a clique, and gang-like behavior was becoming more prevalent. When the issue came up in dialogue sessions, some teachers felt it necessary to eliminate the track system and mix English-dominant and Spanish-dominant students. The mixing of the two language tracks proved successful; a bonus in the change was an improvement in student behavior.

South Tucson and the barrio surrounding Ochoa School have served as the first and sometimes final stop for many who have emigrated from Mexico to the United States, and Ochoa had routinely served children whose primary language was Spanish (and a few Tohono O'odham children). Standard curriculum fare was communicated in Spanish or English, whichever was the primary language of the children in the classroom; however, very little else distinguished one classroom from another. Literacy and language were taught as any other subject, such as history or science.

Decades ago, policymakers had required that students from Mexico or other Latin countries who attended Ochoa and other schools in Tucson learn and speak only English. In the seventies, Title VII of the Elementary and Secondary Education Act (ESEA) provided funds for bilingual education in Tucson—an opportunity for monolingual students to become bilingual and further develop their skills in at least two languages. The then-principal at Ochoa created a bilingual program that she believed addressed this goal and the language and cultural circumstances of the students at that time.

In 1990, when the ECC Project began its work at Ochoa, the language-tracking system was comprised of a monolingual class and a bilingual class for each grade level. When a student enrolled at the school, the class to which he or she was assigned was determined by the parents' answers to three questions: 1. What was the first language the student learned to speak? 2. What is the language spoken most often by the student? and 3. What is the language most often spoken in the student's home regardless of what the student speaks? Students in the bilingual classes were considered Spanish-dominant, and teachers instructed in Spanish. English was the only language used in instruction of students in the monolingual, English-dominant classes. The goal was to have those who spoke only Spanish gradually acquire English and then absorb the rest of the curriculum in English.

Despite the best efforts of the teachers in using this strategy, literacy rates in either Spanish or English among children at Ochoa (and other schools using a similar strategy) appeared to be very low. And, unfortunately, what the children were acquiring in the rest of the curriculum also appeared to be low.

During one of the project's early dialogue sessions, an issue related to the language-tracking strategy arose. The issue centered on the worth of Spanish in comparison to English and extended later to issues of the worth of what the children brought to school—their language, knowledge, and family experiences. Did the children have the "right stuff"? During those early days, the children's "stuff" was viewed by some as not middle-class, not standard, and its worth was questioned.

As teachers in dialogue sessions pursued the issue of language tracking and the worth of Spanish and English, one belief of the teachers surfaced and persisted: There is great value in children knowing both English and Spanish. From time to time, the dialogue group also discussed and inquired into discipline problems, some of which eventually were seen to be connected to language- and class-grouping practices based on the two-track language program.

Before the project began, some teachers had already begun experimenting with a limited mix of monolingual and bilingual students, and after many dialogue discussions, teachers' views were altered. They challenged the tracking system that had been in place at Ochoa about 20 years and began mixing Spanish-dominant and English-dominant students. The fact that team teaching had already become a common practice, and a good number of the teachers spoke both English and Spanish, no doubt made the transition to bilingual classroom instruction easier than it would have been under other conditions.

Following are the experiences of the teachers and students after the principal and faculty agreed to discard language tracking and offer the curriculum to all students in both English and Spanish.

LAURA: When I first joined the faculty at Ochoa, the plan was to immerse the bilingual classes in Spanish in the beginning, and as the students progressed, to teach them increasingly in English to facilitate the transition from Spanish to English. I understood the intention and saw varying degrees of success with this system; it had worked satisfactorily for the people who created it. In subsequent years, however, the principal and nearly every bilingual teacher who initially had been involved with this two-track system left Ochoa for various reasons, and major identity problems among the students began to develop. Each class identified itself so much as an independent unit that the attitudes of the students resembled those of gangs. One group of Hispanic students would call another "wetbacks," or refer to my English-speaking students as "gringos." Students became insolent, defiant, perhaps even incorrigible. The situation became increasingly vehement and volatile, frequently intruding on the classroom. Academics became the thing we did occasionally, because we spent so much time dealing with discipline and interactions among students.

During the first 5 months of the ECC Project, we dealt almost exclusively with discipline and class/school management issues.

ANA: Three years before the ECC Project began, I became a Spanish
    reading resource teacher at Ochoa. I came from a bilingual
    magnet school where I was team teaching first-graders. It was a
    cultural shock to move from a school environment in which staff,
    parents, and students supported the philosophy of bilingual
    education to a school where bilingual education was questioned
    by some staff members and parents, and the Latino students who
    were born in this country were ashamed to speak Spanish. Stu-
    dents were separated according to their language dominance,
    and the separation extended outside the classroom walls. During
    the lunch period and after school, there were many fights be-
    tween our U.S.-born Latinos and the students who had emi-
    grated from Mexico.

    I am pleased to report that that situation is ancient history.
    The problems began to dissipate when we did away with lan-
    guage tracks, began multiage groupings, and began teaching in
    teams. I remember Marianne reporting, very enthusiastically,
    how much more English her students had acquired after she
    began teaming with Becky.

    Children learn from their peers, and what better way is there
    for them to learn a second language than through nonthreaten-
    ing activities with their classmates? In the past, when blocks of
    time were set aside for ESL or SSL lessons and students were
    drilled in a language, students were afraid to take risks and
    there were no significant gains by the end of the year. Now, in
    my first-grade classroom, the Spanish-speaking students are all
    taking risks by speaking English and even attempting to read
    and write in English. The same holds true for English-dominant
    students who are learning Spanish.

    In Delia's and my classes, there are no time slots when we will
    speak a certain language. ESL and SSL drill and practice have
    been replaced with literature, songs, meaningful play-learning,
    interaction in which students have the opportunity to select,
    create, and/or invent their specific learning activity.

    As a teacher/facilitator, I need to be mindful of speaking in
    both languages throughout the day. This occurs very naturally
    for me and I believe it demonstrates a respect for bilingualism.

    I remember one Latino parent who was apprehensive that his
    English-speaking son was in a bilingual setting and did not
    understand Spanish. At first, the child was not very receptive

toward Spanish, but by the end of the year, he would repeat in English whatever was said in Spanish. When a student would read aloud in Spanish, he would attempt to read the book along with the student. He began to respect the Spanish language.

The stigma toward the Spanish language has been replaced in the classroom; students have pride in being able to communicate in two languages.

The linguistic integration throughout the school began during the second year of the project, and Laura saw it as a turning point in her teaching career.

LAURA: I remember that the subject of linguistic integration was discussed among other possible changes at a teachers' retreat. I was sitting at a table with the principal, Elsa, and she was expressing very grave concern about continuing on the bilingual/ monolingual-strand concept. We started throwing ideas around in terms of how to change this process. Because my fifth-grade class was being so difficult, I simply said that I thought we should integrate all of the children in the fourth-, fifth-, and sixth-grade classes. That was the only way I could see to divide the fifth-grade group sufficiently so that they wouldn't have too serious an impact on the school the following year. They were a force to deal with anyway, but at least they weren't in one classroom with one teacher having to deal with them. The integration of classes would divide that troublesome group of students, which I felt had occupied so much of my time that I couldn't pursue changes in curriculum. I mean, those were kids who brought items that could be used as weapons to school. They had girls hide them in case they got caught. They'd say: "You can shake me down. I don't have anything on me." Keep in mind these are fifth-graders.

I can remember sitting in a dialogue session and simply saying—and it was absolutely true: "Either we pursue this and do something definite about mixing these classes, or I'm out of here." I knew it was something that had to happen for me and had to happen for the kids.

DELIA: I felt qualified to teach in a bilingual setting, but, more important, I felt pleased with the "permission" to *be* a bilingual person. When I was in school during the mid-fifties and later, I was among the Latinos who were forbidden to speak Spanish on the school grounds of Tucson schools. I still vividly remember the mixed emotions and trauma I felt when my schoolmates were emotionally and physically punished for trying to communicate in Spanish. How strange life is and what extreme turns it takes. Here I am—40 years later—changing gears, relearning and refining my Spanish and my teaching. I also am learning who I am as a Latina teacher, and I'm learning to discover, love, and be proud of my culture. It's as if the teaching profession is being allowed to develop into what it was meant to be.

SUE: I have been at Ochoa School for 17 years, and the majority of that time the students were divided into two separate strands: English- and Spanish-dominant classes. It was a "cradle to grave" placement and so embedded in their thinking that students in the English-dominant classes were referring to the Spanish-dominant students as "those Mexican kids." It was becoming gang-like on the playground. Something had to be done.

LINDA: Although enrollment in both the monolingual and bilingual fourth grades was primarily Latino, racial slurs were being exchanged and petty arguments were developing among children in the two language-divided fourth grades. Susanna Durón, the teacher in the other fourth grade, and I learned that our students based their definitions of "monolingual" and "bilingual" on the school's practice of labeling classes taught in English as "monolingual" and classes taught in Spanish as "bilingual." When we asked our students the meaning of monolingual and bilingual, they replied that monolingual meant "talking in English" and bilingual meant "talking in Spanish." This led to a discussion about—and understanding of—the prefixes "bi" and "mono."

Considering the children's perceptions of what the school language labels meant, I asked that they raise their hands if they spoke Spanish at home. More than half of my monolingual [English] class raised their hands. We learned that most of us were bilingual to some extent and that the class language labels were misleading.

When Susanna and I began to team teach and mix our Spanish-dominant and English-dominant fourth-graders, I don't remember thinking about whether it would work. We just believed it was the right thing to do. We both perceived segregation of students based on language as an obstacle to their growing and learning. Dialogue was allowing us to think and question our current practices, and when we saw a conflict between theory and practice, we wanted to resolve it.

I believe that children who have a language other than English should be encouraged to develop that language as well as English, and I feel a second language is an asset for people who are predominantly English-speaking. Although I was monolingual in English, my Spanish-speaking teammate was bilingual and always there to translate, and day after day I began to learn more Spanish. The real reward in learning as I taught was that as I attempted to speak more Spanish, most of the students seemed to be comfortable in attempting to speak their second language.

In the following comments from teammates Marianne and Becky, one learns some of the problems they encountered and solutions they found:

MARIANNE: After becoming a team, one of the first problems my teammate, Becky, and I encountered was how to teach two different grades in two different languages. Our second-graders are Spanish-dominant students who are reading and writing in Spanish, and our third-graders are students who are dominant in English. We were both bilingual, but our students weren't. Students kept saying, "I don't understand English" or "I don't understand Spanish." As a team we had to figure out ways to get the learning across. We started pulling all the resources we had, most of which were in English. Then we had to translate nearly everything into Spanish so the information in both Spanish and English would be available in the classroom.

BECKY: I would use Spanish and English in a very natural way so that I was giving the information bilingually. Soon the children were beginning to respond the same way. Initially, Marianne and

I were doing a lot of translating, but I wanted to get the point across that both languages are of equal importance.

MARIANNE: Later, Becky and I began alternating languages—a "language of the week" system, using English one week and Spanish the next. For example, during English week, instructions were given in English and children listened to a story in English. On Fridays, when we had music, we learned or reviewed English songs in Spanish. Also, during math and other activities, children had partners, that is, a Spanish-dominant second-grader with an English-dominant third-grader.

BECKY: When the classes were first combined, students were fighting with each other. It was more or less the Spanish-dominant versus the English-dominant, and our task was to teach them to respect each other, no matter what language they spoke. Now students seem to have learned to treat each other as equal individuals.

Problems of existing hostility between the two language groups of fourth-graders reached a peak. Linda and her teammate at that time found a surprising solution to the problem.

LINDA: During the first year of team teaching, there were many challenges, but one incident will always be remembered. It became known as the "Rock War." Susanna and I had begun to mix students from her fourth-grade bilingual class with my fourth-grade monolingual class. As I mentioned earlier, we had talked about it a lot and felt we wanted to break down the language walls between the two classes. Sometimes I would have half of her class and she would have half of mine—all done very randomly. All indications leading up to the fateful day of the Rock War were that we were doing the right thing.

The incident occurred in early December. It was an ugly fight on the playground between Susanna's bilingual class and my monolingual class, and even the predominantly Spanish-speaking students fought among themselves. There was name calling: "Gringo," "Wetback," "Guacho," "Mojado." A rock was thrown— many rocks were thrown—the war was on with 17 students from one class, 15 from the other. The fight was broken up; however, one child was slightly injured.

Susanna and I were very upset by the conflict, because we had focused so much on the students getting along with each other. There had been many discussions with them about prejudice, and that's what this was all about.

In the days that followed, we pondered over what punishment to administer. Our first thought was to have all of the involved kids sit facing the walls and just write their descriptions, thoughts, and feelings about what happened. The next day we had our scheduled meeting with the ECC Project's principal investigator, Paul Heckman, and he brought up the point that one of the things we were trying to do was to teach children not to hold grudges. If we were going to be punishing the kids and not trusting them, were we holding a grudge against them?

There was talk of separating the classes again, but instead, we did just the opposite. We moved all the tables and chairs in one room and put all the children together at desks in the other room, and we talked. We kept talking about the incident as long as the kids had anything they wanted to say about it. We did a lot of listening, and Susanna and I explained that this was one class; this was the fourth grade at Ochoa, and each of them had two teachers.

I saw children talking more freely about their feelings and getting along in healthy ways after moving through this conflict. Students directed their own learning and soon resolved conflicts with only the help of their peers. We finished the year so close as a class that Susanna and I wanted to stay with the same group of children for fifth grade. As a compromise, we went to the idea of multiage/grade classes and were able to keep some of the children.

The Rock War was a turning point for me, and I think it was a turning point for the students, too. I learned a lot of Spanish that year and interacted with all of the students instead of just my own.

SUE: Linda and Susanna made the initial moves toward the lin-guistic integration of students. They had some really tough times, but they stuck it out. I wasn't really involved at that time, because I had the pull-out English-dominant students in the

Title 1 High Order Thinking Skills Computer Program. But more and more teachers began trying to combine monolingual and bilingual students in the more loosely structured classes, such as art or music.

Full integration of classrooms didn't come until the third year of the project, when the principal insisted on multilingual classrooms. Now that I'm into it, I feel unsure at times, but I'm getting a little better each week. Am I qualified? Who knows? With 6 years of formal Spanish behind me, I've always known a lot of Spanish, but I've never used it. Teachers who have known me for years had no clue that I knew as much Spanish as I do. The kids are wonderful. I don't feel uncomfortable when I make mistakes in front of them, and I hope they will be comfortable with me when they speak the best English they know.

My biggest frustration is in not being able to process information with students when they are really excited and want to share and I can't understand them, or when they need help thinking about something and I don't have the words. The activities I'm doing with the children are purposely very much hands-on to assist all of us in learning to communicate with each other.

LAURA: Although I'm limited in my Spanish, I immensely enjoy the challenge of bringing Spanish learning into my classroom. My English-speaking students integrate Spanish into their learning very naturally and I've followed their lead. I frequently ask for words or ideas to be translated; I encourage students to read aloud in Spanish, especially sharing their writing. Small groups work together in Spanish conversation and activities conducted in Spanish, and presentations to the class are done in both languages if at all possible. Students who are fluent in Spanish have volunteered to help other students in their reading and writing.

I am able to facilitate their learning in both Spanish and English by collaborating with my teammates in developing multilingual curriculum, utilizing our varied strengths and abilities. We also are involved with integrating the native language of our relatively few Tohono O'odham students.

LINDA: My experience in multilingual classes began to some extent the first year of the project with my team teacher who spoke

Spanish. When her Spanish-speaking fourth-graders would come to her, she would encourage them to say the same things to me. The first thing I learned to say in Spanish was *despacio*— slowly, slow down, take it easy. The students began speaking in their less-dominant language in small groups. Students who were known to speak only English were speaking Spanish, and the Spanish-speaking students were practicing their English. When the students realized that both of their teachers valued both languages and were encouraging bilingualism, all of the students—although sometimes hesitantly—began communicating in their second language. That was in the 1990-1991 school year, but I feel it really began to be accepted in the 1993-1994 school year. By then, all things were done bilingually and all children were receiving instruction in both languages. After 3 weeks in the 1993-1994 school year, I had had only one student say: "I can't do that in Spanish." When he said that, I smiled, but before I could say anything, another student said: "That's why you're supposed to sit with people who speak English and Spanish. You're supposed to work together." I didn't have to add anything to that.

DELIA: Although I am bilingual, when we first combined the bilingual and monolingual first-graders, I couldn't really envision how it would work in the classroom. My hope was that students, regardless of race, would learn both Spanish and English and that bilingualism would become valued by all the students, parents, and teachers in the school, as well as ultimately the general population.

My first task was to convince my first-graders of the value of learning two languages, so I talked about the economic predictions for those people who have a second language. That may seem like a high-level topic for first-graders, but it's important that they are offered the opportunity to discuss real issues, and generally they take on a topic at whatever level they understand and accept.

We role-played the situation of a prospective employee applying for a job with me, the employer. It was great fun, and the children were ecstatic about pretending to find a job and answering "yes" or "no" to the employer's questions: "Do you speak English?" "Do you speak Spanish?" Depending upon the response,

I would say: "Yes, you have the necessary qualifications" or "No, you don't have the skills I need to hire you."

I wasn't sure the role-playing message about being multilingual had an impact on them until later in the day when a woman from the Tohono O'odham tribe visited our classroom to present oral tradition stories. Before she could start her presentation, one student asked her: "Do you speak Spanish?" Another student asked: "Do you speak Chinese?" It was as if English wouldn't satisfy their expectations.

On that same day, one of the ECC Project's doctoral students came in to work with the class. Before she sat down, a student asked her: "How did you get this job?" The doctoral student was somewhat shocked to be questioned in such a way by first-graders, but they continued until they got to the question to which they had been alluding all along: "Do you speak Spanish?"

She explained that she was bilingual and that she would not have been selected to work in their school had she not been bilingual. The students seemed satisfied with her response, and I felt satisfied with the point I had attempted to make that morning.

SUE: Before the linguistic integration of classrooms, Laura and I had produced student plays, but only English-dominant students had participated. We were about to embark on a new venture, casting bilingual [Spanish-dominant] students as well. It felt risky, but the results were amazingly satisfactory.

LAURA: Developing curriculum, as we had been doing all along in the ECC Project, can be overwhelming, so as spring approached during the third year of the ECC Project, Sue and I decided we needed to do something familiar. Just as in the old Mickey Rooney/Judy Garland movies, we said, "Let's put on a show." Four years earlier, we had produced "Alice in Wonderland," but then, of course, the script was entirely in English. This time it was to be a bilingual musical, with 12 songs.

One of the ECC graduate students collaborated with a volunteer group of students from my multiage class and another intermediate class to translate into Spanish four of the seven acts of the 35-page script. Students auditioned for the parts they wanted, and we triple-cast all of the main characters. When we gave the parts to the students, there was more trepidation among the English-only students in memorizing lines in Spanish than vice versa.

Perhaps the greatest accomplishment was by a girl who is categorized as "cross-categorical bilingual self-contained learning disabled." She had been mainstreamed into my class for half-days and was determined to play the role of Alice. Sue and I were reluctant, because we knew this was an enormous venture for any student and we wanted to protect her. Ultimately, however, we decided that her desire should outweigh our anxieties.

She, of course, amazed us with her tenacity and resilience. Her performance was applauded by all of the intermediate students at Ochoa. Her reward came in being accepted by her peers. I can't imagine that she'll have too many obstacles in her life if she chooses to overcome them.

Another student in the play, who had a solo to be sung in Spanish, questioned why he was chosen when he didn't speak Spanish. He was one of our most hard-core kids, but he pursued his role and managed to stay in the play for the whole time. He did a magnificent job, and I remember his mom sitting at the back of the room, cheering him on and being so impressed by her son.

In producing the play, we decided to give the kids as much responsibility for it as we could. They were in charge of the music and did all of the synthesizing. They designed the costumes, sets, and props. I kept telling myself to stop doing things and let them do it. Now we're about to embark on a new, unfamiliar play. Sue and I are trying to figure out how to let go of even more of the responsibility in producing it. One thing I've begun to understand is that the more the students do, the more they learn.

DELIA: I find that among English-dominant Latino children there seems to be a status of sorts in speaking more English. When one of my first-graders started school this year, he told me he wanted to write and read in English, because "I don't know Spanish very good." Although the student felt it was the "in" thing to work in English, as he experienced a classroom where both Spanish and English were valued and used interchangeably, he began to read and write and speak fluently in both languages. When I asked about his homework, he said his father helped him with the English because "he is from here" and "my mom helps me with Spanish because she is from the other side."

Another of my students began the school year speaking only English. Now I hear her communicating with others in Spanish. When I was doing guided writing in Spanish with another student, she helped him sound out one of the words in Spanish. She not only is attempting the spoken language but is actually learning the written language.

During the first month of the 1993-1994 school year, I saw phenomenal changes in attitudes toward speaking Spanish. Students always felt English was okay, but the big change is to now see the children communicate in Spanish as well. Initially, they would only use Spanish to translate for another student; now I see them using Spanish in functional situations, not just problem situations. It's wonderful to watch them decide which language they are going to use for a particular situation. I asked one of the students which language he was going to use in writing his "book." He responded "English" and finished his project. Then he came back to tell me he was also writing the same book in Spanish.

There have been other similar incidents. I don't pressure one way or another; the child chooses whichever he or she feels is functional for the moment. One of my first-graders is the only child of a single parent. His mother speaks only Spanish; however, he is seemingly sheltered by a number of female relatives. He had not given me any reason to suspect that he could speak English, yet when a new student, who spoke only English, came to the class, he sought him out as a friend and I heard him communicate very well in English. Schoolwork had not been important enough to him to reveal that he knew both English and Spanish; friendship was the impetus.

Another new student had never spoken Spanish when he came into my classroom. Now he repeats the Spanish he understands when he hears stories or songs or conversation. Recently he selected a book written in Spanish and read it to me in English. Then I asked if he wanted to read it in Spanish, and he said "yes." He read the color words with what seemed like familiarity, and he was so excited to be able to do it. At that moment I felt something very spiritual come over me, as if I had helped him cross over an invisible barrier to a new dimension of communication. He knew it and I knew it. He stared at me with each new word. It was something we both felt by simply reading a book in two languages.

A certain pride in the children is becoming evident as they are learning a second language. One girl was very verbal about not being able to speak Spanish at the beginning of the year. Within a month, I heard her proudly tell some friends during recess: "I speak Spanish too."

Reflections

In this and subsequent chapters the narratives of the teachers suggest what thoughts and actions have changed for these individuals who have been involved in the ECC Project during the past 5 years. It becomes apparent that language and culture are important in discussions of issues concerning school change.

The importance of seeing differences in language and culture as a positive rather than a negative aspect of a school culture emerges in the narratives of the teachers. Subsequently, actions changed as teachers and children saw themselves, including their language and culture, in more positive ways.

Also, Ochoa teachers found that children promote their own and others' understanding and acquisition of a new language when the children are encouraged to be the experts of their own language and thought development. This understanding and language acquisition come about through social interaction and activity in and outside the classroom.

Throughout this chapter there is substantive evidence that changes have taken place as a result of eliminating language tracking. It seems further apparent that many of these changes would not have occurred without all involved persons examining their underlying beliefs about their own language development and views of culture—theirs and others.

What also comes across in the teachers' stories are the struggles in which they were involved—the various beliefs that were examined and altered in accommodating the view that they now express. Some of the beliefs were about the teachers' own views of themselves and their language and the implications of those views for what ideas and actions were shared in the school.

In this examination, conditions were not confused with problems: A different language was not examined as a problem. The language differences in the school were investigated as a condition that existed. The problems had to do with the way the language and culture of the children and families were being viewed by the children and the teachers.

As in most school programs that stratify students according to any one or several characteristics, most students do not benefit from being separated from other students. Laura and Linda discussed how their intermediate-age students became discipline problems. Students used the *presumed differences* to negatively assess their peers.

The changes in student behavior and relationships were an unexpected plus in the creation of multilingual classes. When differences are used to separate and are not honored as strengths instead of weaknesses, negative results occur. In the case of these students, they fought with each other, called each other names, and acted out feelings of superiority and inferiority in their classrooms. Before examining and understanding these stratification effects, the teachers responded to behavioral disruptions like the Rock War with efforts to punish and discipline students. The teachers saw each fight as a misbehavior issue for each of the children involved in an altercation. They sought to change the way these children behaved. In so doing, they addressed the condition, not the problem.

At first, teachers did not see the stratification nor raise questions about it. Over a period of time, dialogues provided an opportunity to examine stratification—what it is, what its effects are, and what explains its existence. Opportunities such as the Rock War provided examples to explore explanations for why children behaved as they did, rather than accepting the conventional explanations offered by the culture of the school.

Two general themes run through what teachers have discussed about these alternative explanations for language and behavior. First, using a principle of heterogeneity rather than homogeneity promoted several new structures and practices in classrooms and holds promise for advancing language development and social development as well as intellectual development among children at Ochoa.

For example, anthropologists and cognitive scientists have noted the importance of social interaction among experts and novices as a condition for acquiring quite complex knowledge and skills, including language. Consequently, providing a mix of language experts and novices in any learning situation will promote such learning among both parties. For the novice, interactions with experts will enhance the novice's knowledge and skills in that language. In addition, as the novice asks for assistance from the expert, the expertise of the expert becomes elaborated and public. The expert becomes fully aware of what he or she knows; having to explain and assist promotes this mindfulness. In our view, then, if students work together in a setting in which some are expert in Spanish and some in English, their reciprocal interaction will enhance each person's language development.

It is not surprising then that teachers report that, even without a preponderance of direct instruction, children who did not previously appear to know a language do know it and use it—and they know what they know. In addition, as students and teachers equally use both languages and discuss their knowledge of the language, both languages become equally valued. The question becomes, as Delia reports, "Which language will I use for this purpose? Which language will permit the best representation of what I want to convey for my purpose?" These questions move away from which language is more important.

Second, when children have experiences in a context that promotes activity and involves materials of various types, children (and adults) will more easily construct meaning, which of course has positive consequences for development of language and thought. Hence, the heterogeneous groups referred to in the discussions of mixing languages in Ochoa classrooms did not primarily listen to a teacher give a lecture and then discuss that lecture among themselves. Instead, each mixed group worked on activities with real materials that provoked meaning with regard to the language being used and enhanced the language development of the children. Teachers also improved their language development by engaging in similar learning processes in which teachers, in some cases, became novices and students. The teachers asked questions about the meaning of a word or the most appropriate phrase to express an idea for the purpose of learning from—rather than teaching to—students.

Finally, as children are sometimes experts and other times novices, they learn that they and their peers each know a lot and can learn a lot from each other. In effect, they recognize each other's competence. When individuals recognize such competence from firsthand experiences, stereotypes diminish and a better sense of self and of others arises. In Robert E. Slavin's (1985) early work on racial desegregation, he discovered that as students worked in "cooperative" groups in highly segregated schools where efforts were under way to integrate different racial/ethnic groups, interracial harmony increased. Students could no longer hold overgeneralized views of their peers as just members of a racial stereotype. Instead, these students had to deal with each other as individuals who have strengths and weaknesses and who belong to one racial group or another.

One explanation for the dramatic drop in fights and discipline problems in the classrooms at Ochoa may have more to do with a sense of competence that each child and adult has developed and the recognition by everyone that others have competence as well. Expertise remains the rule rather than the exception for all individuals in a group, whether they are performing in a play, solving science problems, playing ball on the playground, or writing a story.

Evidence of similar changes in behavior are to be found in the following chapter as teachers reveal their experiences in mixing students of differing ages.

Reference

Slavin, R. E. (1985). *Learning to cooperate, cooperating to learn.* New York: Plenum.

5

Teaching in
Multiage/Grade Classrooms

When Ochoa teachers decided to mix students of different ages, there were no walls torn down or moved in the school building. However, barriers came down between students of different ages and those of different language backgrounds. Various configurations of classes were implemented. Sometimes half of two classes would exchange rooms; sometimes entire classes would exchange classrooms and teachers. Then again, by moving desks and tables, two or more classes could actually convene in one room. Teachers collaborated as teams and planned their class activities together.

As in most U.S. schools in 1990, children at Ochoa were placed in various classrooms according to their age. Each age group, from youngest to oldest, had a grade-level designation: 5-year-olds were placed in the kindergarten class, 6-year-olds in the first-grade class, and so on. Usually, two classes existed at each grade level, and a teacher had responsibility for one of these grade-level classes. Each teacher worked alone with the students for 1 year and then students moved to the next higher grade level. The teacher did not change grade levels but began anew with another group of students of the same age/grade the next year.

The work of the teachers and students and the knowledge and skills to be acquired from doing this work for each grade level seemed self-evident. What the students were to learn was determined by what the district thought to be appropriate and prescribed for children at each grade level. The learning materials for students usually consisted of grade-level textbooks and workbooks, supplemented by copied work sheets. In general, teachers, other educators, students, and parents assumed that these standard conditions promoted student learning and that the grade-level designations assisted in that learning.

I had the view that this standard practice and structure no longer fit in today's world and should be challenged. I discussed my ideas with the teachers during dialogue sessions that focused on grouping practices. For example, I pointed out that Quincy, Massachusetts, replaced one-room schoolhouses with the first graded school in the country during the middle of the 18th century. Quincy created this structure in the midst of a strong industrial base of textile mills in the Boston area, where the idea prevailed that the manufacturing process should be broken up into an assembly line with each worker performing a small set of tasks. This same idea guided the establishment of an "assembly line" for educating children, breaking up the tasks to be mastered by children and having a teacher responsible for educating only for one part of the grade-level products. The same kinds of raw materials would be used, that is, students of the same age.

But times have changed, and so have understandings of manufacturing production as well as how children learn and develop. For example, new production processes focus on the integration of design and manufacturing of a product, featuring an integrated team of design and manufacturing workers who have responsibility for designing and manufacturing the whole product. Each team member has interchangeable functions. Each can do the other person's job. The interchangeable tasks of all members contribute to making a whole product, and these new organizational ideas and practices displace those of an assembly line, where the workers had little say in the design of the product or development of the process. These new arrangements challenge the organizational feature of the graded school and suggest organizing to educate the "whole" child. Children appear to know a lot of "whole" things about the world they live in; they appear to learn from having experiences with whole phenomena. They will more likely understand and know fish by experiencing whole fish in their total context—seeing, touching, and smelling fish in lakes, ponds, and tidal pools, not in seeing pictures of an individual fish separated from its context of living and developing in a habitat.

Also, except during gestation, children develop in complete chunks of larger blocks of time than 9 months; they seem to develop in periods of 3 to 4 years, far larger chunks of time than the smaller time pieces set aside for completion of a grade level. Furthermore, when children move from one teacher to the next each year (grade level to grade level), connections to their peers and teachers, and between their families and the school, diminish.

At Ochoa, I had hoped the teachers would develop an alternative structure that could replace the prevailing separateness and potential alienation posed by grade-level distinctions. In particular, I hoped the alternative would permit children to establish connections to adults and develop attachments to peers and their teachers that would promote their own development.

In the world outside of school, in family settings and neighborhoods, multiage groups of children play together, and in these multiage settings, children learn many concepts and acquire many of the norms of childhood, including language, from other children and adults. However, one adult does not assume the sole responsibility for educating a child or a group of children in families and neighborhoods. Rather, learning in families and communities occurs among a multiage group of children and adults. Both adults and children contribute to each child's learning and development.

In the initial proposal that sought funds for the support of the ECC Project and in preliminary discussions with the Ochoa staff, I suggested the importance of challenging this regularity of grouping students by age in designated grade levels. Ochoa teachers began to examine these existing regularities as a way to understand and change these conditions that for so long had been accepted as normal and necessary.

The dialogues about grade-level regularity involved exploration of ideas I've presented here as well as my hopes for an alternative. As you read through this chapter, many of these ideas will be in the background, and I hope that the reader will also see the effort that teachers had to exert in order to rethink and reenact a new view and structure of how the school would organize children and adults to learn and develop. The following discussions will highlight the understandings and insights—the resolved and unresolved dilemmas that have arisen during the examination of this schooling regularity and the creation of new structures.

DELIA: I remember how teachers used to be stigmatized by lower-grade assignments. They were sort of given "life sentences" to be kindergarten or first-grade teachers—or any other grade level for that matter. Once in a specific grade position, it was very hard to get moved to another grade. It was as if the education system had the idea that teachers had only the same mentality and potential as the students they worked with. That is, a first-grade teacher had the mental capacity to think at only the first-grade level. I always pondered the question that if a teacher starts teaching at, say, the fifth-grade level and moved by chance to, say, first-grade level, does that mean her intellect has diminished?

LAURA: In 1991 my teammate, Delia, and I wanted to do something to integrate her first-grade class with my fourth-, fifth-, and sixth- [intermediate] graders, so I asked my class what they would like to share with Delia's class. The very first thing they answered was the game of chess, which had become an integral part of our class work several months earlier. They went on to list about 25 possible choices, including, interestingly enough, traditional things such as spelling, reading, and math.

Because chess was the first thing they named, and it appeared to be agreeable with everyone, I went to Delia and told her my students planned to teach chess to her 6-year-olds. We both laughed. Half of Delia's class came to my room and half of my class went to Delia's, and the chess lessons started. My kids took partners and sat down with the first-graders and began to teach them how to play.

Meanwhile, four or five of my other students, who had been working in the library at the beginning of class, returned to the room. They were disappointed that they hadn't been there to initiate the chess, so I devised a special project for them to go around the school interviewing people and taking inventory of things in the school. Equipped with clipboards, they were getting organized, establishing their territory of operation, and so on when the principal, Elsa Padilla, walked in on this disarray. She asked: "Did you remember that I'm doing your teacher evaluation today?" (I tell you, as I looked around the classroom, I thought my world was coming to an end. By appearance there was total chaos, with the mix of Delia's first-graders and my intermediate students chattering about chess, and the inventory takers getting organized.) She asked what the children were doing and I told her. She said: "Fine. I'll just sit here and watch."

Although this story is an anecdote about the inherent consequence of having so many people involved in so many activities, it's also indicative of the implicit trust I have in Elsa. She stayed in my room that day, and among the things we observed was a student who had been completely uncontrollable most of the time. On this day, he was teaching chess in Spanish to two youngsters. Neither Elsa nor I had ever heard him speak Spanish before. The students had learned chess terms in Spanish, but he was actually speaking the language.

We had several good experiences with the multiage/grade classes that year, so the following year we integrated the classes for part of the day from the beginning. One of the most incredible things we noticed was how English-speaking students were developing Spanish, and Spanish-dominant kids, without any hesitation, were making an attempt to work in English. Later in the year the first-graders were reading books to my students in English and Spanish. I think the language development was extraordinary.

In the beginning of all of this, I had no idea how to deal with Delia's little kids, and she said she had no idea what to do with my older ones. I now have the feeling that it would really be just fine to have first- through sixth-graders all in the same classroom all of the time, just as they did in the old days of one-room schoolhouses.

DELIA: While walking around the room observing the older students teaching chess to my first-graders, I heard some of the conversations. One of my kids, who is often a challenge, was so happy that he had won a game. I felt really happy that he had been successful in an unaggressive way, and he was good and didn't bother anyone the rest of the day. At another table I heard one of the older kids telling a girl in my class, "Look, if you want to learn this game, it requires concentration."

SUE: I had worked with students in intermediate grades (small group, pull-out) for many years, but only in English. My classroom experience was teaching the third grade, so I was comfortable with that. But things were changing.

I've only been working with second- and third-graders together for 4 weeks, and at this point I'm still questioning how I feel about it. Maybe it's because the classes are multilingual as well as multiage/grade, and the classes are larger as a result of combining the grades. I keep thinking that if I had just the third-grade English-speaking students, I would know what to do, but with all the other pieces, I'm frustrated. I have simple questions about "Do I write all of the instructions and prepare the bulletin boards in both languages?" "How can I get the best from third-graders, who are capable readers, and still respect the second-graders who are at very early stages of literacy—and is it really better to put them together so much?" "Can I really help the third-graders move as far when the classes are combined?"

I agree with combining languages part of the day, but I'm not sure yet how I feel about combining grades. Time will tell.

DELIA: I don't recall having any negative feelings about mixing my first-graders with Laura's intermediate students, and I knew the first-graders were excited about working with the older students. I remember the older kids acted on a nurturing level; they would converse, tease, and relate by reading books to them. They thought the first-graders were "cute," and that's about all they demonstrated the first couple of weeks.

The reading of books went quite well, with initially the intermediate students reading books that the first-graders selected. Then it was decided that the roles should be reversed and the first-graders should read books to the intermediate students. That went well, too. My first-graders were becoming accustomed to mixing for activities with the fifth-graders every week. Furthermore, if Laura or I was absent, the substitute teacher had the option to mix the classes for whatever activities were appropriate. The results were always positive.

As time went by, I was surprised to learn from Laura that some of my first-graders were visiting her after school, just to talk or offer their help in putting things away or other tasks. And they would frequently ask me if they could run errands to Laura's classroom. The interaction they had with the intermediate students and Laura was becoming an extension of their learning. We were becoming a "family" of sorts.

LINDA: When I was teaching only fourth grade, it was apparent to me my first year that textbooks were not meeting the needs of all my students, especially in reading. All of my college training said that it was important to teach to individuals and their needs; it was called "individualized education." My public school experience doesn't reflect this idea. Every 9-year-old was expected to do the same work and learn the same material in 9 months. Changing to multiage/grade classes, I believe, allowed for different learning rates and expanded opportunities for students to make meaning of their learning in a time span that makes sense to them.

In the second year of the project, when intermediate teachers decided to try multiage/grade classes and my fourth-graders were combined with fifth- and sixth-graders, the first thing I heard from the sixth-graders was that they were in a "low class." They thought this, I believe, because I had been a fourth-grade teacher. To be honest, this was difficult to debate, because I had never dealt with sixth-graders before. The sixth-graders also expressed to me that they were angry that they were split up from some of their friends the last year at elementary school. This anger did not subside and changed into gang-like, very ugly behavior. It was very difficult for me to witness this, because I had most of these sixth-graders when they were in fourth grade and thought I had very good rapport with them. They seemed like different people, and this made me question what we were doing. I was extremely saddened and cried often, even at school.

At the same time that we were dealing with hostile student reaction in this multiage classroom, we teachers were struggling with the question of what kind of work we would do in those classrooms. There was no book to tell us how to do it. I found myself pulling away from any innovative teaching practices, including teaching with a partner. I reverted, really, to textbook/worksheet drill and practice. The class went through three guest teachers in that very difficult year. Finally, with the help of Paul Heckman, I developed a behavior strategy that seemed to work. It was based on the idea that kids need to hear clear expectations and need to practice learning a new behavior; however, they will not always do it correctly while they're learning it. I think it boiled down to a question of "caring" versus "control." I first thought I was caring about these angry students, but then realized, through conversations with Paul, that I was really trying to control them. The question I had to ask myself was: "Did I really want to control?" My answer was "no." My goal for the children was for them to control themselves.

Fortunately, this type of student anger was not present in subsequent years.

CHRIS: After experiencing classrooms with multiage children, I really prefer to work in that setting. It's amazing how much children learn from each other. When children have different experiences, they ask each other questions and share more explanations and ideas. The need to talk to each other is built-in, and we create environments in which more learning is likely to happen. It's fun to watch children of different ages and experiences work together during mathematical investigations. Children who have difficulty writing about their strategies get help from children who write easily. They teach each other—often more effectively than teachers can.

It's sometimes hard to distinguish the younger children from the older children in multiage groups. A child's abilities often are more dependent on what experiences he or she has had. When Becky and Marianne and I were working with 7- and 8-year-olds making quilts, this was very evident. Children who had experiences with spatial relationships—by perhaps playing with puzzles or building with blocks—easily cut squares and triangles from cloth and arranged them to match the four-patch design they had drawn. Sometimes it was the older children who had to work hard to recreate their design by moving around the pieces. Experience also was significant in the children who made knots in thread or attempted to sew even stitches; success was more a result of experience than age.

An advantage that teachers found in working with classes of various ages was that they often would be with the children for 2 or 3 years. For example, a teacher who previously had taught only 8-year-olds in third grade, often would know the child from the time he or she entered school if that teacher had teamed with teachers of 6- and 7-year-old children. In the past, teachers had only the 1 school year to work with a child; they felt they did not have time to really get to know their students as well as they would like or to develop meaningful relationships with the children's parents. The children and their families did not form strong connections to the teachers or the school. When teachers were with children in subsequent years, they also had an opportunity to evaluate their own work by learning what the children had retained of their previous year's classroom activities.

LINDA: I like having kids for 3 years, because I have a chance to see how they grow in that time period. I know that whatever these kids are lacking, there's no one to blame except myself. It's a lot of responsibility, a real eye-opener.

BECKY: Some years ago I had kids for 2 years and I loved it because I could see all their growth. At that time, someone brought up a question about a teacher's areas of weakness. You know, we all have weaknesses, and if the children don't advance to another teacher, they'll be void in the teacher's weak areas, whatever those areas might be. I think that's where team teaching, especially in multiage classes, becomes important—that is, providing your weaknesses are different from your teammate's weaknesses. Teachers can draw from each other's expertise, and the children benefit from the expertise of both teachers.

LINDA: During the third year of the project I had sixth-graders in my class who had been with me since fourth grade. I had an incredible sense of pride in this group of boys. They were leaders in all areas.
Although there were some objections from the older students when we began combining grades and teachers were staying

with a class for 3 years, that has changed. Now, most of the students, and parents too, like having the same teacher for 3 years. That's how it works, my teammates and I have students for fourth, fifth, and sixth grades. By the time they graduate from sixth, they've been with me for 3 years. I would very much like to continue teaching multiage classes; however, I want a curriculum that allows for a wide range of abilities and skills—in other words, contextualized teaching. The relationships that have developed between students, parents, and teachers lead me to believe that this is a positive change.

I also feel it provides conditions for teachers and parents to work together for the children. The only other time when I have experienced such positive communication between parents and myself is when I taught more than one child in the family.

LAURA: It's interesting for me to realize that at this point (the third year), I don't even consider a four, five, six combination as a multiage/grade class. The symbiotic relationships among my students are natural and very positive—certainly more natural than assuming that students develop in 9-month increments. Actually, from the first day, an outsider could not discern a fourth-grader from a sixth-grader. And now, if someone asks, the students sometimes don't remember either.

My enthusiasm has increased with each year. I cannot imagine ever returning to a single-grade-level class.

LINDA: If teachers stay with their students for 3 years, rather than just the 9-month school year, it's easier to work and talk with their parents. At the end of the third year of the project, four boys graduated who had been in my class for 3 consecutive years. One of the boys was dominant in Spanish, and Spanish was spoken in his home. I had met his mother many times during the past 3 years, and we did our best to communicate, but it was difficult with my limited Spanish and her limited English. When I saw her on graduation night, she said, crying, "Thank you so much, *por* Eduardo." That meant a lot to me.

All in all, I believe combining the grades provides students with room to grow. There is not a 9-month expectation of students; instead, they have 3 years to reach the expected goals. For many, this means achieving at their own pace, instead of falling years behind or being labeled for special education.

The following conversation between Chris and Laura was recorded shortly after the decision was made for students to stay with the same teachers for more than 1 year. In it, they compare experiences since their participation in the ECC Project with the years when they were teaching traditionally.

CHRIS: Years ago, when I first started teaching at Ochoa, we kept the kids for several years. One frustrating part of it was that every year the kids couldn't remember what we had done the year before. I couldn't point a finger at another teacher for this lapse, because I had been their teacher. Of course, I was teaching traditionally at that time. I remember one student who had always been very quiet during the 3 years she had been in my class. She came up to me one day and said, "Mrs. Confer, I've kept every single paper that we've ever done, every single worksheet." I had this sinking feeling in my stomach, but I asked her how tall the stack was. She said: "It's up to here," indicating about 3 feet. I had this image of all the trees I'd destroyed and wondered if all I had taught was in that stack of papers, rather than in the minds of the students.

LAURA: I moved up from fourth to fifth grade with classes a couple of times, and you're certainly right. I would say, "Come on, we studied this last year." And they would answer, "We did? Are you sure? I don't remember."

CHRIS: All in all, keeping the same students for several years is good, and if we didn't have these experiences we would probably say, "Things are fine. Why change the way we teach?"

LAURA: After developing our own curriculum, the responses were different. At the end of the second year I asked the class for an evaluation of what they liked and what they didn't like and what they remembered of our studies that year. It was very interesting; I had responses on the papers about things that we had done even the year before.

Reflections

In this chapter, teachers have discussed how they embraced several new ideas and tried out new grouping structures for educating children at Ochoa. Laura's realization that her older students enjoyed playing and teaching chess to the younger students encouraged Delia and her to see other possibilities for mixing ages of students in other activities. But first they had to abandon the idea that older children can learn, teach, and play chess and younger ones cannot. In addition, they also had to give up the belief that teachers teach and students learn. In their examples of playing chess and reading, older students taught younger ones and later younger students taught older ones.

Furthermore, as Sue suggests, she and others also had to confront a belief that before they did something like mixing ages, they should know what they were going to do and the probable outcome. Instead, they had to launch an activity in which the character of the project would not be known and the result would not necessarily be guaranteed. As Sue also shows, giving up a practice such as grade-level designations does not happen easily. Many other aspects of schooling suggest the reality of an existing regularity and deny the credibility of an alternative. As Linda pointed out, students also have a built-in sense of gradedness. They also will struggle against new regularities, because they too experience them as an unknown and have anxiety when the unexpected happens and/or ambiguity increases dramatically.

Yet when Laura and Delia, for example, had sufficient experience over time with multiage groups of children, they described two conclusions: They had positive experiences with these new arrangements and they cannot always discern who is older and younger in the mixed-age groupings. The fact that they report a positive reaction to a new circumstance may encourage a view that the anticipation of a new option often generates more anxiety than what follows. Often, we find that our worst fears are not realized.

In addition, Laura and Delia reported that when they have experienced children in mixed-age groups, they could see no differences among children of different ages and they could not tell from appearance or behavior who was in fact older or younger. Such a finding fits well with the early research about same-age class groupings of children. When researchers examined achievement and other measures of maturity among a group of same-age children, more variances existed among same-age children than among children across ages. As a matter of fact, the differences among same-age children increased as they progressed through the grades. John I. Goodlad and Robert H. Anderson, in *The Non-Graded Elementary School* (1987), offer a rule of thumb that the difference in achievement is twice the grade designation of a group. For example, in a typical sixth-grade class, a 12-grade spread in achievement can exist in any one subject area.

What this discussion points out is that differences are the fact of human beings, and even when institutions such as schools have sought to diminish the appearance of variance, the fact of differences looms large. Children have knowledge, wants, ideas, and interests, albeit different knowledge, wants, and so on. And these differences promote the advantages of mixed-age grouping as a dynamic learning community is created in which experts and novices both teach and learn.

Reference

Goodlad, J. I., & Anderson, R. H. (1987). *The non-graded elementary school* (Rev. ed.). New York: Teachers College Press.

6

Creating Contextualized Curricula

An early concept of the ECC Project was that students learn more in the context of their "real lives" than through prescribed, standardized curricula. When teachers at Ochoa gave up their "textbook teaching" and turned to contextualized teaching, it was a real challenge. Most of them turned to the process of inquiry—first asking students to reveal what they know and then creating study units on the students' questions or their own questions. As in the process of inquiry, the roles of teacher and learner (expert and novice) often are reversed. As the study unit is developed, students do the work of scientists, mathematicians, writers, and other professionals in problem finding and solving and acquiring knowledge and skills in basic subject fields.

Various and broader ideas about contextualized teaching/ learning have developed in the ECC Project as teachers examine existing—and create new—conditions for learning in their classrooms and throughout the school. Ochoa teachers have changed many of their ideas and practices about their work and the work of their students. In this sense, they are teaching in a manner that brings new meanings to contextualizing. Through interactions with community and families, as well as through student inquiry, they are focusing their teaching/learning on the real lives of the students.

They are promoting student learning in the community by encouraging students to examine various aspects of their community as scientists, mathematicians, historians, artists, and the like. And in so doing, students actually do science, mathematics, and other subject fields and can therefore begin to understand these naturally occurring events.

In investigating community phenomena, adults and children use what they already know to learn more about a phenomenon. Children have knowledge and skills when they come to school, and the teachers are building upon that knowledge. Because students know the most about their own community and neighborhood, they increase their opportunities to learn more as scientists, mathematicians, and so on, by using their existing knowledge. Neighborhood events and family circumstances also greatly enhance the base for student learning, and children's interest in these events and circumstances encourages them to have questions that will guide their learning investigations. Student motivation also is increased if they find they can improve their neighborhood by making changes in features of their community through their work as scientists, historians, and the like.

As learning is contextualized, teachers and students are brought together in a learning relationship; each person in this relationship makes explicit what he or she knows about the subject matter, and as they make their knowledge explicit, all persons learn and benefit from this relationship.

Some individuals (child or adult) know more about—and have more expertise in—an event or circumstance than others. In consideration of this, an important condition for learning arises that differs from the traditional student-teacher relationship in which the adult is the teacher and the child the student. In this context there is an expert-novice relationship, and neither teacher nor student exists in traditional ways. The particular delineation of being called an expert or novice depends on who knows more and who knows it better, not who is the child and who is the adult and who has the certificate. As students are engaged in contextualized learning, the roles of student-teacher (novice-expert) can be reversed (expert-novice).

In both novice-expert and expert-novice relationships, Ochoa teachers and students develop questions and work in investigating the students' real world as scientists doing science or other experts in any of the traditional subject fields (reading, writing, history, mathematics). Teachers believe students are smart and know a lot, and the knowledge of the students is acknowledged by the teachers.

Of course, dilemmas remain because of the ambiguity and messiness of doing this work, in which one kind of expertise is being replaced with another. Teachers are no longer the ones who explain everything and tell students what to do; instead, both teachers and students acknowledge student expertise. Such an important development challenges teachers' senses of themselves and their traditional work and roles.

DELIA: Historically, teachers all had the same philosophy and the same basic techniques for educating students. There was a sense of security in knowing that for generations school had been consistently taught a certain way; smart students "got it" and the not-so-smart students didn't. Teachers were very predictable people; the more robot-like they became, the better they were regarded in the total system. Every year the curriculum was the same, the materials were the same, and the expectations of students were the same. Lesson plans were used year after year without any changes other than the names of the students. The teacher always had the answers, or if he or she didn't, it wasn't taught. The teacher—never the student—assumed the position of expert, while the student's job was merely to be the recipient of knowledge. Any expertise or reasoning skills of the student lay dormant.

MARIANNE: It doesn't seem very long ago that we were writing our lesson plans right from our manuals or teachers' guide. For years, we used those manuals like a bible. The manuals/teachers' guide told us what to say and when to say it. We also had math and science curricula we used to make sure we were teaching everything we needed to teach for that particular grade level. It was almost as if we couldn't think for ourselves. Contextualized teaching is like a release from bondage.

LINDA: I have always believed that contextualized learning was the most lasting and meaningful. Although I had not put a label on it, I was practicing it in my classroom before the ECC Project came to Ochoa. When I strayed from the adopted texts, I always sought permission from the principal. My plans were always okayed, so maybe he or she also knew that it was the right thing to do. I was relieved to hear that the only thing that made sense to me (contextualized learning) was valued by the ECC Project. I know when I was in school that I didn't learn from textbooks, work sheets, or rote memorization, and, almost subconsciously, I didn't expect my students to learn that way either.

LAURA: One of the motivating factors for me in developing curriculum is the fact that we are involved in the complicated and enigmatic age of technology. I am one of the teachers who has been interested in technology since the early eighties. One of the school district people I admire most once said, with regard to calculators and computers: "When the Model-T Ford became affordable to almost everyone, people did not keep horses just in case the automobile was a passing fad."

Although I am committed to the utilization of technology, I don't believe it alone can take the place of teachers or fix what's wrong in education. However, not to use it is a travesty and a tragedy imposed upon some students today. Also, the misuse of it is overwhelming. Students do not need electronic workbooks. Some software is simply "drill and kill" plugged in.

My students know more about computers than I do. In word processing alone, they can make graphs, spreadsheets, and even slide presentations. They're able to do many things with which we adults are unfamiliar or afraid. But the important thing is that computer technology also requires many skills. Students must be able to read, write, and solve problems in order to use a computer.

It is not sufficient to tell students that they'll need to be able to read, write, and solve problems when they grow up. They are already doing these things. In fact, the isolation of reading and writing had always seemed to alienate students. Their attitude then and now seems to be that it's not worth the bother to learn to read in order to answer questions on page 36 or some other page. But if they want to access Classroom Prodigy or other software or write an important letter, reading and writing are seen by the students as essential skills. Even Nintendo becomes a learning device if a student wants to get to the next level of "Super Mario."

At Ochoa, we don't have constant access to technology, but we do have a lab of 30 computers, which we use several hours a week. I feel this is classroom time well spent. It's almost as if technology in itself is a motivation for students to learn many basic skills.

CHRIS: As I think back about all the time that we spent creating definitions in Essential Elements of Instruction, I just laugh. I remember trying to create the right definition for *patterns* for children to repeat back to me. So what? It doesn't matter. Children repeating my definition of *pattern* has nothing to do with learning. In all probability, one of the turning events in my life as a teacher was the pumpkin business, when I was teaching with Delia. In one of the teachers' weekly dialogue sessions, we had been questioning how much children already know and what they want to know.

Then, back in the classroom, the learning experience about pumpkins started with a first-grader's question: "Why is there a button on the bottom of a pumpkin?" Pumpkins were brought into the classroom and pumpkin research began. When a pumpkin fell from a table and broke, the children were astonished to find there was no juice spilled. The project continued with the mother of one of the children showing them how to cook the pumpkin and make *empanadas* [turnovers; see Chapter 10, this volume]. As she worked, she intuitively explained that the juice of a pumpkin is in its pulp and is released when it's cooked.

Subsequently, the children were asked which of two statements is true: "A pumpkin has *no* juice" or "A pumpkin *has* juice." Half of the students agreed with the first statement, the others with the second statement. As discussion went on, the second group explained that although a pumpkin does not have juice sloshing within it, it indeed does have juice in the pulp. The pumpkin experience continued to planting the seeds, a study of soil, the need for water and sunlight.

At one point, a rather quiet, withdrawn boy spoke up and explained that he had opened seeds and that they have baby leaves within that grow through holes in the seed into larger wing-like leaves.

Later, Delia and I examined the first-grade science textbook to see what it would have presented to these children. The science book said three things: (a) plants need air, water, soil, and sun; (b) plants are green; and (c) plants are everywhere.

Had I been teaching alone, I'm not sure I could have realized the validity of this teaching/learning experience. In addition to Delia and me, there was another resource teacher present, so there were three adults asking questions and watching children. That adult support was very important. At a later time, Delia and I reflected on our teaching about pumpkins and wrote an article about it. I think allowing the time for reflection increases the power of what we're doing.

BECKY: Sue and I conducted a third-grade classroom unit on insects that inspired great interest among the children as well as ourselves. It all started while the two of us were enrolled in a children's literature class at the University of Arizona. This class had stressed the process of inquiry. In other words, starting with a question that may lead to another question or may lead to an answer that leads to another question. That, perhaps, was the best part of the insect unit, because it took us in the direction of the students' questions.

SUE: We started the insect project by finding out what children already knew, and we learned they already knew a great deal about the subject. We made a graph of the children's feelings about insects, told stories about personal experiences, and began to weave a web of what was already known. Some invaluable scientific help was provided by a person from the University of Arizona's Department of Agriculture, who supplied the class with many different types of insects, as well as some good advice and support.

Each day in class we tied the project to literature by reading aloud something that pertained to insects, whether an article, book, choral reading, fiction, nonfiction, or poem. As a theme, we stressed the cycles of life and the interdependence of all living things. Points of focus included the concept of living things being free and the importance of flowers in the life cycle of an insect. The children became familiar with the scientific names as we classified arthropods and used the proper vocabulary in our discussions. It was obvious that the children felt powerful in owning those difficult words.

About 50 fiction and nonfiction books were chosen by the children, and through independent or paired reading, they found answers to their questions that developed through the project. Each child kept a journal in which he or she recorded the findings of the research and new questions as they arose.

Live insects were brought into the classroom; we had isopods, mealworms, Madagascar hissing roaches, and others. The children became scientists, observing the insects with microscopes and touching them, if they wanted. And always, they recorded what they saw or felt. Teams of children became responsible for each insect, and they built insect "houses" out of tennis ball containers in which they could collect insects at home or on the playground.

As the children posed their questions, they put them on a large chart, ultimately dividing into groups to research the five questions that were most important to them in their lives. They had all contributed to a chart that defined how they could learn things, and it was up to each group to decide how they would investigate their questions and record their answers. Among the choices for learning were books, videos, real-life scientists, individual experiments, and so on. An entomologist from the university was invited to visit the class, and she brought a video about insects and showed other facets of her work. By the time she left, several students were convinced they wanted to become entomologists.

Ideas for carrying the insect project into other areas were suggested and discussed by the students. These included music, poetry, art, writing, computers, construction, quilting, puppets. Becky and I felt it was an indication of their hunger for creative expression that they signed up for only three: construction, art, and puppets. Whatever they did in each of the three areas was required to relate to insects.

Becky and I continued to expand the insect inquiry and were able to retain student interest in doing so. A mathematics study came from one child's question: "How far can a grasshopper jump?" We discussed what a scientist would do to answer such a question, such as count, measure, time, observe, question. . . . Together we designed a grasshopper experiment. Groups of children recorded the distance of four grasshopper jumps and used snap cubes to find the average of the four. They created a graph on which to record the findings; they used a spreadsheet on a computer to turn the information into a bar graph; they then compared the grasshopper jumps to human jumps by measuring broad jumps performed by four students. During their required $2\frac{1}{2}$ hours each week in computer lab, students created, edited, illustrated, and printed their own insect stories and turned them into a book. They also created covers for their books and "fantastic insects" for an art show.

Becky and I concluded that the insect inquiry project was extremely successful and we were reinforced by the powerful and positive response of parents to the class presentation on family day. [In Chapter 10, there is dialogue that took place between parents and teachers after the insect unit was completed.] Although as yet there are no tests for student assessment of such project work, I feel the project strengthened skills in mathematics, science, reading, writing, word processing, art, and research. And all of this came from students' questioning minds about a subject that is real to them.

DELIA: Outside speakers have always been viewed as effective in classrooms. Traditionally, a speaker would make his presentation to a quiet class that would applaud when the presentation was finished, and then all would be over. Today our 6-year-old students are not content with that format; they expect more, they want to talk, they want to ask questions.

Our team had invited a young Latino who is a mechanical engineer to be a guest speaker for our first-graders. He had recently patented an apparatus that launches spaceships. The day before he came, our class discussed the prior knowledge they had about mechanical engineering. It was not surprising that the children associated a mechanical engineer with an automobile mechanic—perhaps because we had recently finished a project on cars and trucks and other vehicles. So, shortly before the speaker arrived, we simulated an invention experience that a mechanical engineer might encounter. We gave the children a piece of paper and pencil and asked them to draw an invention that would make a bicycle go faster. Their responses ranged from wheels of many sizes to unusual designs for horns and baskets.

As it turned out, after the engineer showed a video and told the class about his own invention, he talked about an invention that began with a problem of creating a bicycle in which senior citizens and disabled persons could safely and effectively carry merchandise. Bingo! Our kids related to that example perfectly, because the bike and the need were both in their prior knowledge.

The speaker described how his coworkers brainstorm and dialogue all the time and write down the ideas they come up with; he pointed out that all ideas are respected as springboards for other ideas. Bingo again! As a class, we often discuss a variety of mutual concerns and interests. He then showed them some tools of his trade: measuring and drawing devices, textbooks, and other books. The books were great, because he opened one to a page that had illustrations, graphic representations, and computer representations. After he talked about the academics and skills that need to be learned in school, one student asked, "Do you write a story about what you do?" The guest took out his science log, which contained his own graphs, illustrations, narratives, and numbers. His log was a perfect example of tying all facets of his work together, just as in our classroom work we bring together reading, writing, math, art, and data collection in books that students compile.

Finally, the guest speaker simulated with the students a brainstorming session with his professional colleagues. He presented the problem of a bridge that gets dangerously icy and slippery for vehicles. The students and we teachers were enthralled with this real-life enactment in solving the problem: What can we do about the bridge? He diagrammed the bridge and listed ideas the children suggested to solve the problem. As it turned out, one of the girls actually suggested a solution for the problem. The exercise emphasized the beauty of teamwork. The ability to work cooperatively to solve problems is a skill children must develop to succeed in life.

The engineer mingled with the kids like an adult with other adults. They responded by showing him their computer graphics and reports they had made in the earlier vehicles unit. They shared with him their protractors and other tools they had used. The guest talked about engineers who design cars, bridges, highways, and medical equipment. And he talked about those who design toys and landmarks, such as Disneyland. Needless to say, that last one was a clincher.

The mechanical engineer was a godsend; he confirmed our belief that what we are doing in the classroom is right. The presentation became an interaction as students became problem solvers together. And as one of my teammates said: "He left our students the hope of one day being successful and respected—the hope of being useful in society and helpful to their families."

ANA: I always have a skeletal plan in mind for what might take place throughout the school day, but there is no assurance that it will be carried out, because I strongly believe in the process of inquiry, following the students' ideas and questions. Before I was engaged in the ECC Project, I spent countless hours writing lesson plans with objectives, only to cancel them because of unanticipated interruptions, and sometimes I would get very upset when I had not "taught" all of the lessons for the day. Those were my "imposed" teacher plans—plans I imposed on my students. The children were not included in the planning and negotiation of their own learning as they are now. I have discovered that the actual learning processes that are structured as activities are the essence of learning, not the activities alone. Before, I would make the decision on whether the child had actually learned. Now, each student reflects on what he or she has learned.

SUE: Offering choices to students seems to me to be a vital part of learning. For example, I believe that to experience success and make choices about their futures, students need to read, but what they choose to read and how they will pursue reading may be negotiable. The same is true for mathematics and communication skills. The element of choice comes in when we involve students in the questions of what to study, how to study, and when.

The work of Howard Gardner in "multiple intelligence" has encouraged me to think about learning in different ways. He believes that people learn in at least seven different ways but usually prefer one or two. Schools have traditionally emphasized the verbal intelligence area, so students who are stronger in one of the other areas, such as the bodily/kinesthetic or interpersonal modes, have suffered, because in most classes all students have been required to respond in the same way. One opportunity for choice might be for all students to decide in which medium or genre to share their knowledge. The teacher might say, "I need some way to tell what you know," and help the students not only think about different ways to share their knowledge but also help set the criteria for evaluating their responses.

During the fourth and fifth years of the project, Laura and I, with another teacher, Lina Valdez, experimented with giving the children more choices about what and how they wanted to learn. Lina worked with students who chose to develop the Lot Project [discussed later in this chapter]; Laura organized a Construction Project; and I offered a Quilting Project. Students had their choice of projects, and we teachers worked with the students in finding the math, science, and reading contained within each area. In quilting, for example, in addition to learning the art of quilting (appliqué, piecing by hand, crazy patch, nine patch), we also read literature about quilts, looked at geometry (angles, tessellations), and observed how culture is reflected in the quilts of a people.

One young man, who was notorious for being absent a lot, began to attend class regularly, and I think that in part it was because he had the opportunity to follow his love of model building in Laura's construction group.

BECKY: A study unit that seems especially interesting for my 7- and 8-year-olds each year focuses on Native Americans. Initially, it was to have been a unit that might lead into the Thanksgiving story. Beginning with *Annie and the Old One,* written by Miska Miles, the unit branched into weaving—at first with paper and then with cardboard looms. The children got so involved in weaving that they made a life-size loom out of wood that was found out in the desert. It looked magnificent and was very authentic. From there the children began looking into the origins of wool and then a comparison of natural dyes and man-made dyes. They even made some of the natural dyes and tested to see whether the natural wool or the store-bought yarn took the dye better. Ultimately, the children tried weaving on a real loom and were very excited about their endeavor. This unit took a longer time than I had planned, but all along it followed the interests and questions of the children.

During this time, we invited Yaqui and Tohono O'odham people to come into the classroom and talk about their cultures. They shared songs, stories, and some artifacts of their tribes. I remember on one occasion, a very quiet Tohono O'odham child joined in the songs and dances that his tribal representative performed. He seemed to shine with pride because he knew these songs, and his own language was being acknowledged. Then, no longer the shy and quiet child, he proceeded to teach his class-mates how to count in his native tongue.

Other interesting activities have evolved from this Native American unit, although it changes from year to year, depending upon the various interests of the children. One year the children decided to write their own coyote stories and stories about their families, which they developed into puppet shows. At other times, after researching Native Americans, they have made moccasins, recreated homes, and learned songs and dances that are indigenous to Native Americans.

This study has turned out to be a real favorite of mine because it takes a different turn each year, based on the children's interests and creativity. Rich learning can be traced to Native Americans, and this unit allows us to reach out into the neigh-borhood where much of this knowledge lies.

One of the biggest, schoolwide, contextual teaching experiences began with Chris taking an intermediate class for a walk in the school neighborhood and challenging the students to talk about the problems they saw. Trash-filled vacant lots were among the most noticeable, and there began the children's efforts to engage in a clean-up program that was initiated by neighborhood adults. They wrote stories and made and handed out flyers that urged people in the community to join in a designated clean-up day.

Ultimately, 30 of the elementary school students attended a Tucson City Council meeting and asked—in both English and Span-ish—that a city-owned lot near school be donated to the school district for an educational purpose.

Linda's class took on the task of addressing the City Council:

LINDA: As a result of a dialogue session, I had adopted the rule of *inviting* children to do some study tasks, rather than *assigning* or *ordering* them to do things. So I invited students to write speeches to present to the Tucson City Council, pointing out that we should have the vacant lot for educational purposes. That was on a Friday; on the following Monday, 10 students returned to school with diagrams and speeches (some in Spanish and some in English). With the help of Councilman Steve Leal, we were placed on the City Council agenda.

With sack lunches in hand, 30 children and 5 adults boarded a city bus for downtown Tucson and walked to City Hall, where we ate our lunches. When we went into the council chambers, the kids were awed by the new and different surroundings. They studied the name plaques on the tables, the printed agenda, the pictures of past mayors, the videocamera, and the signs posted on walls and doors.

Each student who prepared a speech was heard (although we later learned that the Council had previously determined the outcome of our request). The children were praised by the Council for participating in the government process, and we left City Hall in victory.

With the lot now deeded to the school district, and with the guidance of Lucia Hoerr of the Tucson Audubon Society and some financial help from the Junior League of Tucson, plus involvement of parents and several teachers, plans were advanced for the children to transform the lot into a small urban park and wildlife habitat.

The challenge of this project was gigantic in the minds of teachers as well as students. Teachers had no experience in such a project, and there was too little evidence of the finished habitat to make it seem real in the students' minds.

Nevertheless, as soon as the lot became officially theirs to develop, teachers began using it as a contextual teaching tool. Some students measured the lot and figured fencing, and some studied the soil and identified plants that might grow in the hard desert earth, but the reality of the habitat was—and still is—a very long way off.

LINDA: As some money came in for development of the lot project, new questions came up: Who would manage this money? Who would decide how it would be spent? How could I get children to have a voice and be involved in this? In other words, how could I get children involved in as much of this *real* work as possible? The solution was to have some students investigate different ways to keep records while others brainstormed lists of materials that should be purchased. Classroom dialogue and negotiations began.

As the months rolled by, some students and teachers were anxious to get on with the project and make physical changes in the lot, but others wanted to take their time, maintain certain standards in its development, and do it right the first time. This dilemma is revealed in a conversation between Chris and Laura:

CHRIS: You know, some plants can't survive under certain conditions, and if we don't plan it right, it's going to be a problem for that plant and the lot. It's a long-term project. Maybe if it weren't so distant or [if it were] something smaller like planting a tree, the kids could see immediate results.

LAURA: I think understanding the necessity of standards and valuing consistency will become apparent to the students and teachers when they become actively involved and begin to notice things are changing and that they're actually making a physical difference in that piece of property. I think it's very hard for everyone right now to try to develop something that's in the imagination. It's all real, but it's real head stuff, and that's a totally new area for kids to be coming from.

CHRIS: Maybe it would be good to plop in the watering system and start doing something.

LAURA: I've got kids who are just dying to go down to the lot and get their hands in the dirt. It doesn't sound like a big learning experience, but it's going to be.

CHRIS: A lot of questions will come from that [such as]: Why is the ground so hard?

LAURA: Yes, how can we make it softer? Obviously there's a reason why nothing is growing there. I think probably it's simply that the ground is too hard; it won't allow a seed to develop. What do we have to put into it? A lot of questions will develop from our own knowledge and our allowing kids to develop questions and find the answers. I think the physical aspect of the lot may be where the kids will begin to develop knowledge and understanding about things that grow.

CHRIS: Another thing that I've run into is that there is a lot of written material on desert plants, but it's all in English. Students in the plant group really want to learn things, but they are Spanish-dominant, and there is nothing for them to read.

While some teachers wrestled with the lot project, others were involved in the effectiveness of the process of inquiry in determining curriculum. Becky found the process an effective way to teach in the context of students' real lives. She also saw it as an effective tool in diminishing behavioral problems.

BECKY: Questions posed by the students reveal their hopes and concerns. We did a lot of inquiry during the third year of the project, and we're going to continue it in several different areas because it really works. Kids were looking up answers to their own questions; they were experimenting; they were engaged. In the past, I could put up a question, but if they had no interest in the subject, they had no interest in pursuing the answer.

In addition to its advantage in teaching, inquiry helps in maintaining discipline. We used to have so many behavioral problems, but we have virtually no problems during the time the children are engaged in inquiry. They love it. I think it's a real answer to discipline problems. Kids have to be engaged—engaged in something that interests or affects them.

SUE: When I talk about the ECC Project and my new teaching practices—no textbooks and that sort of thing—outsiders always ask questions, such as: "How do the children learn to read or write?" "How do they get the literature instruction that I got when I was in school?" Perhaps a poetry unit that I did with Laura will help provide answers.

I have always had the need to explore literature in depth with children. I love words and language and I wanted to introduce my 9- to 12-year-olds to that world, to help them develop their own appreciation and understanding of poetry, poets, and writing and to share it with others. In one class, reading poetry led to sharing it with others and then to writing it. Language preference was no problem, because there are large collections of poetry available in both English and Spanish.

Poetry was the focus of the unit, but each child was provided an opportunity to exercise individual preferences and efforts. We began by starting poetry journals, a place where the children could collect their favorite poems. This way, each could explore the types of poetry he or she liked the best, and it allowed participation at individual levels of capability. They had the option of working in English or Spanish.

We set up an "Author's Chair," where a child would sit when reading favorite poems in his or her collection. Laura and I also shared our favorite poems and talked about our favorite poets.

Then students were asked to explore the life and works of one single poet or poetess, one subject in poetry of the student's choice, or one genre of poetry, and to make a collection. Selections ranged from poets Shel [cq] Silverstein and Langston Hughes to topics such as horses and dogs, Native Americans, African American poets, bears, and poems that are specifically in the category of humor.

Finally, students were asked to experiment in writing their own poetry. Although poetic structures were identified, one of the rewarding parts of the project was the outpouring of self-knowledge and self-expression when they were given the opportunity to write about what they know and their inner feelings. Most of the students were eager and willing to do this, especially some of the sixth-grade boys, which surprised both Laura and me. Many seemed to realize for the first time that they could put their emotions on paper and share them with others.

DELIA: One project for my 6-year-olds was on balance. What is balance? We talked about it and wrote about it. We discussed where balance is in our classroom, our homes, on our playground, in our world, and in ourselves. Then during play-learning, the knowledge the children had about balance was manifested. They showed us balance in their somersaults and in their use of blocks and construction toys, and in creations made of clay. They showed us balance as they danced. One child said, "I can balance on one foot. I can balance a book on my head"; another said, "Pencils can balance on different things like a table or your finger." Throughout several days children shared their findings with other students; they would listen to each other and ponder. The knowledge of balance was in their minds, and from there it manifested itself into activities that related to the whole child.

ANA: Another learning demonstration with the 6-year-olds involved a study of sound. We began by asking "What is a sound?" We all closed our eyes and listened for various sounds. As children stated what they felt sounds were, Delia wrote their responses on chart paper, and both of us continued to emphasize that we were proceeding on this study the same way a scientist would proceed. We were "working as scientists." I took up a guitar and played on the strings. *"¿Qué pasa con las cuerdas de la guitarra?"* "What's happening with the guitar strings?"

"Se mueven," one boy said. "The strings wiggle," said another. "It goes so fast we can't even see it," announced a third child. I took the opportunity to use the word *vibrate* for *wiggle,* and through inquiry we deducted together that the sound is made by the strings moving against the air.

The next demonstration of sound involved my hitting a glass of water with a spoon and then continuing to hit the glass as water was removed. The class could determine the differences in the pitch and arrived at the conclusion that air, water, and glass move fast and make the sound. Later students demonstrated the difference in a sound created by blowing air into a glass bottle and blowing air across the top of a bottle. Finally we divided into groups at tables with a variety of objects, and the children invented sounds with the objects that were there. Then, with a great deal of enthusiasm, they explained their "sound inventions" to the whole class. I'll have to admit it was a relief to my ears when our work as scientists ended and the children went outside to play, but all in all, the message of sound was learned.

CHRIS: Becky Romero, Marianne Chavez, and I wondered what mathematics 7- and 8-year-olds would naturally bump into if they were to make patchwork quilts. We began by taking advantage of the children's expertise in sewing and had those with that experience teach the others. They made different things from scraps of old material. Several of them made little cloth bags, which they treasured; one little boy slipped pieces of a special cookie in his bag, which he guarded closely. Whenever the children sewed, peace filled the room. Even very active or angry children were drawn in by the contentment and quiet that descended. It's too bad that "helping others" and "feeling at peace" are not part of the curriculum; both are important.

We invited an accomplished quilter to come to the room to show the children several of her quilts. They watched closely as she showed them how she made stitches, and as she sewed, she explained that mistakes were part of the process. "You don't need to get mad, you just fix them," she said.

We teachers showed the children how four-patch quilt blocks are made, and working as partners, they drew an array of 2×2 squares and then decided whether to leave them whole or to divide them diagonally.

We posted the patterns on the board and talked about the shapes that emerged, all the while using standard geometric terminology. We noticed smaller shapes that [when placed] side by side created larger shapes; we came to appreciate that geometry is part of the world around us. We were developing understandings that the National Council of Teachers of Mathematics (NCTM) believes is essential for children to have.

The children decided that each group should select two colors and then make a class presentation explaining why they thought those were the best colors. The final decision was made after each child voted on a class graph. The children gathered and analyzed data (another recommendation from NCTM) to make a real-life decision that they cared about.

The next step was to cut fabric squares to match their paper patterns. Many children struggled with such questions as: "Which way does the triangle need to point?" "Should the square be above or below the triangle?" "How did we make that hexagon, anyway?" Many children experienced a challenge to their spatial sense.

The children had a mathematical problem to solve as they decided how to arrange their 18 patches to create a rectangle. Most decided that a 3 × 6 arrangement would make the nicest quilt, although a 2 × 9 and a 1 × 18 were possible, too. Our quilts turned out beautifully, and we celebrated by having a quilt-tying party, much like the quilting bees we had read about in books.

How could we assess this experience beyond what we had observed as the children worked? We asked the children, and they created criteria for "a good patch," which helped me see the activity in a new light. A good patch, they pointed out, laid nice and flat. All the shapes' points came together evenly. The stitches were small and all the same, and the shape should remind you of something you like. They wrote evaluations of their own patches according to those criteria.

I wanted to know more, so I interviewed a few children. I especially remember talking to one boy. He liked his patch a lot because it reminded him of what he called "Chinese dice." His uncle had bought him some and had taught him to play a game with the dice. The boy looked down as he explained that his uncle had died. "They put him in the ground in New Mexico," he said. It hit me once again that we never know just what the children are experiencing. It's important to touch base with children one-on-one to find out.

What did I learn as a teacher? I was confident that we would encounter important mathematics, but as the activity progressed, I saw mathematics emerge that I had not anticipated and I learned to verbalize what I saw. I came to understand in a new way that I as a teacher value what I've come to call "life skills": things such as helping others, knowing that it's okay to make mistakes, finding ways to deal with sad things that happen to us, feeling proud of accomplishing a difficult task, and appreciating a thing of beauty that we ourselves have created.

SUE: Something I worry about is how to make sure there is valuable content in the program—that children are setting and maintaining high enough standards. If choices ensure nothing more than keeping the students happy and engaged, I'm not sure it's enough. If, on the other hand, their curiosity and investment in their self-chosen investigations spur them to reach higher and farther, then we have succeeded in many ways. One thing I need to keep asking myself as a teacher is: "Are the children 'bumping into' the things they need in order to succeed?" If not, how can I alter the learning environment to ensure that they do?

Reflections

During the past 5 years, the teachers have used contextualized teaching in various ways to promote learning in their classrooms. In so doing, they have developed new work that advances learning for students as well as themselves. Although the teachers' thoughts and actions could be described by some readers as illustrations of good instruction, I choose to discuss these developments of new work as examples of powerful *conditions for learning*.

The newly invented schoolwork developed as a result of many inquiries by the teachers, the principal, and the project staff about the views on which they based their old practices 5 years ago. They had to examine and understand their old views and ultimately distrust them enough to entertain new ones. As they sought further understanding, their newer ideas made greater individual and shared sense and overtook the older ones as guides for developing new practices.

The teachers didn't know about contextualized teaching as an instructional practice or strategy; they learned about it and created its many features. In fact, they had to first challenge the very idea of instruction based on decontextualized teaching so that they could see the importance of learning as a result of context and experiences.

Decontextualized instruction has inherent, underlying beliefs about a teacher teaching something that can be removed from its context and presented to learners without regard for its context. Yet contextualized teaching has its basis in very opposite ideas; the context conveys meaning and suggests knowledge and actions that might differ in a different context.

Instruction denotes that the teacher teaches mainly what the student is to learn and has little to do with what the individual student thinks and does in a learning experience of real material, people, and events. Contextualized teaching sees the importance of social interaction among expert and novice with real materials, people, and events, as well as the messiness and unpredictability of what the individuals knew before they entered the context (experience) and the variance of what each will know and understand during and after the experience. Instruction plays a very small role, if any, in learning through experience and in context.

The Ochoa teachers have described a number of key features of their invention of contextualized teaching. Their invention, however, has certain conditions that make learning from a context and/or real experience more likely:

1. Teachers and students focus on what they each know and understand about any phenomena that they will investigate. In other words, contextualized teaching advances self-knowledge and self-expression. Each person expresses what he or she knows. To do this, each involved person must be aware of what he or she knows and then that knowledge must be expressed. Delia and her team members and Becky and Sue, respectively, illustrate the importance of both self-knowledge and expression when they discuss what their team did before the mechanical engineer came to their classrooms and before the study of insects was begun. The children expressed what they knew about engineers—they were automobile mechanics. In addition, when the engineer asked the children how they might solve the bridge problem, the children expressed what they knew and thought about. Finding out that children know a lot about insects and graphing that knowledge also promoted learning.

2. "Investigations" in a context and several features of these investigations also further learning. For example, in what the teachers discussed, the children and the adults expressed their interests and questions (thereby promoting self-knowledge and self-expression) and then they negotiated the questions or interests that the group would explore together. Chris told of children exploring

a 6-year-old's question about pumpkins; Becky and Sue described what happened after their children had agreed to examine the question, "How far can a grasshopper jump?"

In addition, the investigations take on the qualities of "real" science as the investigators [the students and their teachers] approximate the activities of doing science. Becky and Sue's group designed a grasshopper experiment. Members of the group measured, recorded, and analyzed the average length of a jump, going so far as to use a spreadsheet to assist in their data analysis. They reported their findings to an audience by creating their own book.

3. In their investigations, children and adults used materials and mental tools, which also appear to promote learning. I already mentioned the use of measuring devices, graphs, and computer spreadsheets as some examples from Sue and Becky's experiments. Ana used a real guitar to explore sound with her team. Chris and Becky used quilts, needles, thread, and rulers as they made quilts and examined the patterns that they created.

4. Several teachers mentioned the significance of encouraging reflection, which is another vehicle for encouraging self-knowledge. Ana distinguishes between what she did in the past, when she would determine how much children had learned by what they did, rather than on what they expressed about what they had learned. She and others routinely urge children to reflect on what they know and what they think and learn. In addition, Sue highlights the importance of representing self-knowledge when she describes how the children wrote about their inner feelings during the poetry unit. Students represented their feelings in written form, in poetry (an important way of representing knowledge and feelings).

Nevertheless, although these conditions appear to promote learning when students and teachers investigate phenomena in context, several issues remain. Among them is the fact that contextualized teaching encourages messiness and unpredictability. What will the children and the adults investigate? What interests and questions will guide these investigations? And how long will these investigations take? In past practice, most questions such as these had been answered in advance. Good instruction defined the parameters and the knowledge to be acquired. Good teachers found out what students did not know and then created opportunities for them to make up these deficiencies. When students quickly acquired this knowledge, their teacher could view him- or herself as more effective, and the faster a child learned the material, the smarter the child appeared to the teacher.

Contextualized teaching encourages very different circumstances. The issue remains how to continue to promote these kinds of learning opportunities for children when older ideas prevail throughout an educational system. Teachers have expressed here the tension that exists when taking on such unpredictability and messiness. Two dimensions of this tension seem most apparent:

First, traditional assessment and testing seek predictable responses, which presume a neat and tidy conception of school knowledge to be taught by teachers and learned by children. As Becky and Sue reported, no tests existed that could help them know what their students had learned in the insect unit. And, given what Chris and Delia discovered about seeds and what the textbooks wanted their children to know, the standard material neither challenged nor took advantage of all that their children knew before, during, and after the pumpkin investigation.

Second, continuing to dominate the schooling world is the view of books and textbooks as the primary sources of knowledge from which children and adults should learn. Educators often confuse textbook or book knowledge with research. True, a book conveys knowledge, and when individuals read it, they gain meaning of that knowledge; however, the knowledge of books exists independent of the reader. Views underlying contextualized teaching are that (a) books provide an occasion for individuals to bring their own meanings to a text and to further know what they know and (b) individuals play back and forth between experiences they've investigated and analyzed in the context of their real lives and the knowledge of what others have found out and recorded in books; this process repeats itself in further investigation of the acquired knowledge and well characterizes the idea of research.

7

Managing Student Behavior

"Control" has traditionally been the key word that teachers, princi-pals, parents, and other adults use when they talk about the behavior· of children. Ochoa teachers have taken another tack, working on conditions that promote good interaction of students with their teach-ers and classmates, changing curriculum, and building self-worth. In turn, their work in these and other areas promotes the students' sense of responsibility for their own actions and encourages a system of self-regulation.

The results of a number of studies show that the schoolwork of children consists primarily of seat work, listening to the teacher, and telling back to the teacher what they have read or heard. The ECC Project promotes the idea that significantly changing student and teacher work will add value to the educational experiences of the children and help them to fully achieve in school and benefit from what they have learned.

The project makes this assumption because the existing adult work in schools appears not to promote healthy adult interactions among teachers and/or between and among children. Traditionally, teachers appear to focus on what they believe other teachers, the principal, parents, and children want or expect of them. An assumption prevails that good teachers know what others want without hearing it directly. For example, there appears to exist a view that all teachers know what classroom behavior everyone expects of children and that everyone shares the same views. Yet little time exists for them to regularly discuss and examine together their daily work and seek others' views. Therefore, teachers must infer what their colleagues want from them and what these colleagues think of the work that they do in their classrooms.

The norm of taking care of children looms even larger. School administrators (as well as parents and virtually everyone else) expect teachers to take care of the children—to keep them in order, to figure out schoolwork that will compel and interest them, to provoke questions and answers that will unravel their mental puzzles, and to resolve the many interpersonal issues that arise among children. In this regard, then, the teachers truly are the workers in schools, and the children have little to do that's relative to the teachers' responsibilities. In this sense of taking care of others, schooling does not promote the mental health and well-being of either the adults or the children. At this point, I want to emphasize that I distinguish between "taking care of" and "caring about" someone. Make no mistake, caring and compassion among adults and children exist in project schools—and I hope all other schools.

The project has further assumed that student behavioral problems will diminish when caring and compassion exist and when the work of students has compelling aspects of (a) promoting self-regulation, (b) fostering student interests and questions, and (c) figuring out ways of accomplishing investigations focused on those interests and questions.

During the early stages of the project, student behavior emerged as an ongoing topic of dialogue sessions. Initially I believed, and still do to some extent, that a group of teachers will focus on student behavior in the early dialogue sessions, because this topic may keep them a safe distance from having to express what they really think and believe about other topics on which dialogue may focus; they fear revealing too much of themselves. However, as members of the Ochoa dialogue group continued to examine their daily practices and explanations for these actions, especially with regard to student behavior, personal beliefs soon surfaced and with them other deeply held feelings and ideas about students and what they did or did not do in classrooms.

At first, when student behavior came up in dialogue, I tried to help—to take care of the problem. I suggested that the teachers and others discuss their theories of behavior modification and reinforcement theory. Despite the fact that such theories do not directly promote self-regulation (and have other difficulties as well), I nevertheless thought that if everyone had such strong feelings when children do not behave the way teachers want them to, an easy solution rests in understanding and implementing theories of reinforcement. (In a limited fashion, this theory does appear to promote desired behaviors.)

I was wrong on two counts. First, the teachers had little interest in examining these theories of behavior modification in relation to what they experienced in their classrooms, and second, the problem that I identified was not the real one.

As a result, beliefs about student behavior and control became topics of examination in dialogue sessions on several occasions. In the best of all worlds, a teacher—and any other adult (or child for that matter)—will feel better if someone responds positively to his or her request. Certainly, the children did some pretty outrageous things to each other and sometimes to teachers, but what could account for the very strong feelings of anger that the children's behavior aroused in the teachers? When children fought, the disappointment and hurt of the adults about this fighting seemed to be based in something beyond a wish for children to take care of themselves and not fight. One basis for such feelings appeared to be about the teacher's loss of control. When children did not follow teachers' requests, then teachers were not doing their job. They were not in control, especially because administrators, parents, and other teachers expect each teacher to control the children assigned to his or her class. The examination of control seemed important in light of the teachers' feelings of anger and disappointment.

Part of the reinvention process consists of examining the practices presently under way in schools, including explanations underlying these regularities, and creating new practices based in new explanations. Addressing and discussing control and the behavior of children in school illustrate the importance of developing new explanations that replace old ones as the basis for new practices and strategies. In the case of discussions in dialogue, we examined and discussed these distinctions and urged "caring and compassion" in preference to "taking care of others" and "self-regulation" over "other-regulation." These newer explanations appear to have provided an impetus and better basis for new practices and strategies that promoted student development.

Behavioral problems have significantly decreased at Ochoa, as you will read in this chapter, but they have not evaporated, nor will they in the future. Human development appears to engender and require some conflict; therefore, we have sought to promote child growth and development through attention to behavior and conflict, rather than to focus on eliminating disruptions and conflict.

You will read about these new explanations and others that provided insights into practices that had held sway in the school for a long time and had not been questioned by teachers until they were discussed in dialogue. These new insights also provided the foundation for developing new practices and strategies, which the teachers also discuss in this chapter dealing with how they now handle behavior problems and conflict among students. Finally, you will hear concern for child growth and development, rather than control and order, in what my colleagues share in this chapter. A greater chance now exists at Ochoa to enhance children's achievement, and what and how they will benefit from education, than when the concern in the school focused on order and control.

LAURA: Before participating in the project, I had become a very disciplined, controlling teacher. This was the expectation of my colleagues and the principal. The belief was that a quiet room was a good room. We "knew" lots of learning was going on in a quiet room. Although my classrooms didn't become much noisier over those years, the students' productivity and attention diminished. The harder I worked at controlling my fifth-graders, the less meaning and understanding seemed to be accomplished. Also, the students seemed to become more devious, underhanded, and nasty to each other. While I was successfully raising their ITBS scores, I was going crazy with all the discipline problems.

Student self-regulation sounded like nice words in an impossible situation. Initially, I certainly didn't believe that this was possible. I went through a lot trying to "make" my class be self-regulating and self-disciplined. It didn't occur to me that self-regulation and self-discipline couldn't be controlled by me.

LINDA: Managing student behavior was a constant topic in dialogue sessions. One of the controversies involved kids coming into the building before school began. Teachers spent most of the before-school morning telling children to go outside. When the children asked "Why?" most teachers said they needed that time before school started for uninterrupted planning. I had a problem asking kids to go outside during cold months, because some of them came to school in shorts and sandals (which were okay as the day warmed up). After much discussion, the majority of us felt that maybe it wasn't so important for the kids to go outside. They could come in and use computers, play games, or do work. Some teachers promoted this idea and some didn't. This demonstrated to me two obstacles in changing class management: One is that history, tradition, or whatever you might call "what has always been done" is very strongly held in the minds of teachers, even new or young teachers; the other is there is an ever-widening gap between theory/research and practice.

DELIA: We call some of our class discussions "business meetings," and the children love them. An example is one day, when two of my 6-year-olds found a syringe in the playground sandbox. This led to a very effective business meeting in which some children shared very poignant experiences they had gone through in relation to the use of drugs by family members and friends. It was an opportunity to talk about family life, drugs, germs, prevention.

The so-called business meetings call for the children to be responsible for their own actions and share responsibility for others in the class. The process seems to be building self-confidence. After a very long and intense business meeting one day, one girl said, "Okay, we're tired. We should now go outside for a break. Who wants to vote? I'll count." And she did just that. Working together to meet their immediate needs, the kids all marched outside to play.

MARIANNE: College students who are preparing to be teachers seldom, if ever, receive training in managing student behavior.

That's just not part of the course work. Yet, skills in managing behavior are essential if learning is to take place. Because there's no preparatory course, teachers must learn these skills from their own life or schooling experiences. It requires constantly trying different approaches, because what works with one student may or may not work with another.

I've been fortunate in working closely with Elsa, the principal. In addition to serving as acting principal when she was on medical leave a few years ago, I am the designated principal whenever she is out of the building for any reason. In preparing for that role, I've been able to observe how Elsa interacts with students and deals with various discipline problems. She is there as a facilitator when there are problems or conflicts between students; she's there to problem solve rather than talk to them. Sam Gallegos, the student counselor, uses a similar technique, and the students have a lot of respect and admiration for both of them. They've both been excellent role models for me.

During the time I served as acting principal, I tried to follow their example. Each student involved in conflict had the opportunity to tell his or her side of the story. Then I would ask the students to talk about the problem together and tell the adversary how he or she felt. This approach is very time-consuming but effective. Sometimes I would ask the children to determine what the consequences to them should be, and I found them to be very fair and sincere in their responses. Penalties generally ranged from being detained in the office and losing play time during the lunch period, or writing a letter of apology to the other student, to telephoning the parents and informing them about the misconduct.

LINDA: I remember one of the first experiences of settling conflicts in my intermediate class. One student tripped on the playground and blamed another student. When they returned to the classroom, they were all discussing it. I asked the class if we needed to talk about it and how the matter could be resolved. The class decided that the tripped student and the one being blamed should stand in front of the class and tell what happened. I decided to sit in the back of the class and just observe, although it was very difficult for me not to get involved. But, after all, I hadn't witnessed the event.

The class began to ask questions of the two students and the questioning went on for about 30 minutes. At one point, the student blamed for the tripping was asked to go stand behind a bookcase. After he did so, the tripped student was asked: "What color are his shoelaces?" He answered "Green," which was correct. I suspected this question was to prove the boy guilty, but, instead, the questioning continued for another 15 minutes. Finally, a girl in the classroom asked: "Did anyone get hurt?" They all agreed no one had, to which the girl replied, "Then why don't we just forget it?" That seemed okay with everyone, so we returned to our class work.

Conflicts after that were settled in a much shorter time. During future class meetings I would ask if there were any conflicts to be brought up, and this system worked very well, or at least I perceived it as such, because there seemed to be fewer conflicts during the class meetings.

ANA: Children often choose their own ways to resolve conflicts and often the ways they choose are fairer and far more democratic than ways an adult would choose. For instance, voting has proved to be a popular way to make decisions among some of the 6- and 7-year-olds in my class. At the beginning of the project's fifth year, there were three beanbags [chairs] in the library area of our classroom, and the children were pulling, tugging, and arguing over them. During a discussion period, I brought up the concern. One girl became the problem solver by suggesting that we pick names each day and take turns using the beanbags.

In spite of this, use of the beanbags continued to be a problem. I asked the whole group whether they wanted to stop using the beanbags altogether. Some said yes and some said no, all at the same time. There appeared to be total disagreement. Then one of the boys in the class said: "I guess we're going to have to vote on it," an activity that had resolved an unrelated issue the day before. The girl, who had earlier been the problem solver, became the self-appointed teacher, went to the blackboard, and began to organize a very simplistic form in which the votes could be cast. The boy, also assuming the role of teacher or expert, helped in counting the yeses and nos. I just stood back and watched democracy at work, led by 6- and 7-year-olds. The final vote was 11 to continue using the beanbags; 6 votes against.

Use of the three beanbags continued until the following month, when the class decided to give one of the beanbags to another class. More discussion followed and the students decided the line leader each day would pick two names of students who could use the remaining two beanbags. The students went further in deciding that they would be used only during reading and rest time.

Certainly, it was a minor issue, but the students' initiative in resolving the problem and the manner in which they did it were very gratifying.

DELIA: Manuel [not his real name] is a new student and a challenge in my class of 6-year-olds. He is volatile and physically aggressive and justifies his actions by blaming others as the instigators of conflicts. Substitute teachers don't want to come back to the classroom because he slaps and kicks at them. Teachers, parents, and students all complain to me about Manuel because I don't have trouble getting along with him. I often wonder if his older siblings abuse him at home and if they too are victims of abuse.

The child uses profanity constantly, and on one particularly difficult day, the children and we teachers decided to have one of our "business meetings" to discuss behavior problems. We sat in a circle, identified the problems, and proceeded to discuss them. One boy said it used to bother him when someone called his sister a "bad" word. He said now he just ignores the name caller because "I know it isn't true." Another child said that when someone is being mean or using bad words, "I get up and move somewhere else." One boy who earlier in the year had spent many days in denial of any wrongdoings offered Manuel his own form of advice: "Manuel, don't lie." Manuel had his head down looking at the floor; he said nothing; he didn't squirm or scream at the class or walk out of the classroom, all of which are typical responses for him.

None of the children insinuated that Manuel was a bad kid, only that his behavior was unacceptable to the group as a whole. In our business meetings, the children express their hurt feelings and their disgust, but they never judge or label another child. They are honest and offer encouragement for behavior modification and, above all, hope to the perpetrator. I suggested that we all show Manuel that we wanted to be his friend and asked those who were interested in being his friend to stand. They all stood—even those Manuel had hurt during the day in a physically aggressive or verbally abusive way.

Manuel is an angry and hurt child, but he can learn to think things through in his classroom. He doesn't know he has so many options, but his school friends can make him aware of survival skills.

LINDA: Even in schools that aren't making efforts to change curricula and teaching practices, student behavior is usually an issue. In the dialogue sessions we often talked about managing student behavior and the gap between research and practice. Paul Heckman contended that if the students' study tasks or activities were engaging enough and teachers used consistent reinforcement of appropriate behavior, there would not be problems. In dialogue we talked about student self-regulation and how we might encourage children in this direction. I thought I had a handle on the theory of reinforcing children's good behavior, but I needed to figure out "engaging." My first effort was what I thought was an engaging task; however, only about 75% of the class was engaged. There were still those other kids who stood out behaviorly and always seemed to be "unengaged"; they were always the same kids. When I asked them what was engaging or interesting to them and began offering choices, the 25% who had been unengaged came along. This seemed to be one piece of the puzzle in managing student behavior. It's difficult, though, to be thinking about managing behavior of a few students while you're dealing with 30—and often more—other growing little persons.

Also, I think honest communication and interaction might be another piece that works in managing behavior, and part of that is being honest with myself and the children and admitting that I don't manage their behavior, they manage themselves. I can't *make* anyone do anything, certainly not prepubescent 11- and 12-year-olds, and I never pretend to. Every person is responsible for himself or herself. In the classroom we talk about behavior openly and from the viewpoint that we're all learning. Just as baseball players get good at baseball by practicing, children get good at managing their own behavior by practicing. It's a high goal for 12-year-olds, but shouldn't we reach high?

I was always wondering how to prepare the kids for a future we don't know about. I somewhat resolved that question by expecting the kids as well as myself to do and be our best. One must realize that each person has a different best. It takes personal discovery to identify your best; it's very difficult to discover oneself.

At a Title 1 math workshop, I heard a teacher describe a system for students solving conflicts. She said there was a clipboard at the front of her classroom, and when a child was having problems, he or she could write his or her name on the clipboard and the class would discuss the problem at what they called a "class meeting." I took this idea back to my classroom and we decided to try it. We didn't use a clipboard, but we did have meetings and spent a lot of time talking about personal problems as well as community and school issues.

At one point, I felt very confused in trying to concentrate on student self-regulation while I was negotiating meaningful curriculum, authentic parent and community involvement, and alternative assessment. I was overwhelmed and wanted to concentrate on one thing at a time, but then I saw that all of these things are connected. I shared my confusion with the kids. I don't think they understood the whole tangled mess, but they seemed to see my confusion and appreciate my honesty. I think that made it okay for them to express their confusion when they felt it, so I began to approach class management with honest communication. I was happy to see the kids open up and do the same. They solved some long-standing conflicts and gave each other advice on how to handle things. It felt like a very open, honest atmosphere, although it wasn't always easy. I wanted to share this discovery with the other teachers and assumed it would work for them, too. I wanted to prescribe honesty for everyone, but I soon learned I had to control my enthusiasm for this concept. If I believed prescribed or imposed strategies didn't work for the students, what made me think I should impose my style of class management on other teachers? I found that some teachers were uncomfortable with such honesty. They were wonderful people, but just not ready for that much self-exposure. In my classroom, however, self-regulation became the important tool for behavior.

I found that having guest teachers once a week was an opportunity for kids to practice doing the right thing. I explained this to my students and we talked a lot about it. Did it always work? Honestly, not always, but it was one answer. Let's face it, behavior is a tough issue.

MARIANNE: We had finished a study of a thematic unit, and I asked the children what they would like to study next. As they started to walk to their seats to generate their lists, Armando began pushing Miguel (not either boy's real name). So I stopped what we were doing and decided this was something that needed to be addressed before going on. Lately, Armando's behavior had changed. He was different; he was fighting, hitting, and pushing other students around. He was becoming more defiant, and this aggressive behavior was becoming more and more evident. I tried talking to him, keeping him during lunch, taking away his free time, but nothing seemed to work. He spent a great deal of time daydreaming; therefore, his assignments were always incomplete.

Finally, I called Armando's mother to see if I could find a reason for this change. She told me that the boy's grandmother, with whom he had been very close, had recently passed away. His mother felt that Armando was angry with his grandmother for leaving and with God for taking his grandmother away.

After some thought, I decided that our next study theme would be feelings and emotions. The librarian provided me with all sorts of books about children and adults losing a pet or a loved one. We did a survey to see how many students had lost someone they loved—a parent, brother, sister, grandparent, even a pet. We found that about 10 students (about half of the class) had experienced having someone die. Our school counselor came in to talk to the whole class about feelings. He shared with the class what he had felt when he lost his mother. The children wrote stories on the computers about their losses and their feelings; students brought to class and shared pictures of their parents, grandparents, and pets. Later, they drew beautiful pictures to illustrate their stories.

I also brought in pictures of my brother, who had passed away 8 months earlier, and the children seemed surprised to see that teachers are also human and that children are not the only ones who have to deal with some of the hard things in life. The difference, of course, is that some children have to deal with these emotional things at a much earlier age.

SUE: Students today live in a difficult world. They are forced to make serious choices at an early age; they come to school street-wise. Some bring a lot of anger and frustration into the class-room, which surfaces in belligerent behavior with each other or violent behavior on the playground.

As a teacher in a pull-out program in which I worked with small groups of students and had the option of sending a disrup-tive student back to class, behavior was never an issue. We did things the kids enjoyed (especially during the HOTS Program when computers were new), and I had time to interact with children individually. But now, as a classroom teacher, a different set of circumstances has made me face a different reality.

Early in the fifth year of the ECC Project, when the behavior of several students in my intermediate class began interfering with the other students' right to learn, the classroom became an uncomfortable place to be. My immediate reaction was to tighten down, become more autocratic and get things back in control. My attitude (if only implied) was "You will do such and such, because I am the teacher, and I know what's best!" In my head I knew I was into a power struggle and that these kids had a lot more staying power than I did. I also knew that although the punish-ment/reward system might work for a while, it would never result in the long-term attitude changes I desired.

At this point, in a traditional school setting, I might have had help from the principal or a school counselor. At Ochoa, I had that same kind of help, but I also had a teammate and a group of teachers in dialogue who had faced these problems before and were willing to not only listen supportively and offer advice but also to take action. In one instance, it was volunteering to take these students into their own classrooms for short periods—to allow me, as well as the other students in the class, to take a deep breath. Because I was working with a team and we had begun allowing the children to make choices, some of my behav-ior problems spent part of the day in another classroom, thus my teammate helped share the load.

When students who are dealing with a lot of negative feelings enter school and find a classroom filled with a lot of prescribed textbooks and a set curriculum that is not related to their lives, they become even more defiant. I believe I need to make the curriculum responsive to their interests. I know that when students are given a choice about what or how they will study, they have a stake in the learning. By involving the students in the selection of and implementation of curriculum, they assume ownership for their decisions—even their decisions about behavior issues.

LAURA: The first year that we implemented multiage and multilingual classes for the intermediate students, they had a lot of questions about why we were doing this to them. Students felt torn from their friends, and although the environment wasn't hostile, it was foreign. Some students from the monolingual English strand were upset because I was a fifth-grade teacher, not fourth or sixth, so how was I going to teach all three grades? Others were concerned about my lack of Spanish. So we began having class meetings to discuss such questions—discussions about their real world and not what I controlled.

Something I discovered on a limited basis, years before the project, was that the engaged student is not a behavioral problem. Through the years I had been using more and more materials such as Marilyn Burns's Math Solutions and GEMS science. It seemed that as long as we were doing those things, I had virtually no problems. I was sure there must be ways to accomplish the same thing in reading and writing. That's what the ECC Project allowed me to begin exploring.

During the past 5 years, many students have demonstrated abilities and skills that would not be obvious in a classroom of tests and textbooks. The most interesting thing is having the other students recognize those individuals and acknowledge them in class. Self-esteem seems to be directly proportional to self-discipline. Although some discipline problems still occur, they seem to be primarily about specific individuals and not class management.

My students are in charge of our room and all the materials and equipment in it. They also have access to the cabinets that contain all of the bulletin board materials and supplies. If they can't find it, we don't have it. We do have some loss of materials, but I believe it's far less than what we experienced when I was in charge and they supposedly didn't have access.

Recently, several things happened that were very disconcerting to me. Somewhat unconsciously I began to enforce things in the classroom. The more authoritative and autocratic I became, the more problems we had. I expressed my concern in a teachers' dialogue session. As we talked, I realized that I was the problem: Students were reacting to my trying to control them. The more I tried to control them, the more negatively they reacted. Obviously, I can't go back to the old idea of my controlling student behavior.

DELIA: One morning, just as school began, I had a pressing request to provide a somewhat lengthy piece of clerical information for the principal. It required working on the computer in my classroom, and time was short. I asked my first-graders: "Can you wait for me while I finish this information to give to the principal right away?" The kids looked at me as if to say "Of course we can get along without you." (Asking that question in the first place was definitely the traditional teacher in me, but I felt guilty in not doing the regular routine right away. Also, the traditional teacher in me expected chaos, which added to my anxiety.) I simply went about my job on the computer, and without direction, one boy went over to the attendance folder, picked it up, and started reading the students' names out loud and recording absences. By this time he had everybody sitting cross-legged in front of him and listening as he sat in the "teacher chair." Then one girl came to me and asked for a dry erase marker, which I gave to her. She posed a question to the class: "Who is wearing pants?" She wrote the question on the dry erase board, with help from the class on the spelling. Then she drew a graph on the board and the students got in line to write their responses to the question in the proper place on the graph. She guided those who weren't sure which side to write on. This was a child who started school only a few months earlier, saying, "I don't speak Spanish." On this day she was explaining the graph in both English and Spanish. They tallied the count and together worked to spell the words for a summary sentence, which is the "story" that summarizes the graph. Her next effort was a made-up song in praise of the class, with some la-la-las thrown in, and she even added clapping to the song at one point.

Before she sat down, she announced that one of the other students was going to read two stories to the whole group. When he started reading, the children started choral reading with him, which he had not expected. He said, "No, I will read it alone to you." Another student commented, "They can all help you." This was followed by a little dialogue and negotiation, and the reader got a little affirmative reflex on his face and said, "Okay, we can read it together." The reading began, but it wasn't finished when the class we team with came in for our regular combined session. I had been typing on the computer the entire time. None of the students asked, "Am I doing it right?" No one said, "I'm bored." No one said, "I can't do it." No one said, "I can't read." The children had a job to do and they felt empowered to do it.

LAURA: When kids make choices about their activities, they're engaged in their own process—in their own learning. That, in itself, is a commitment. They are not only actively learning and gaining knowledge, but I found in my own class that it eliminates a lot of management and discipline problems.

Reflections

The teachers have discussed the new ideas and the resulting new practices that they have created, during the past 5 years, in managing student behavior. The idea that appears most useful has to do with self-regulation. Students manage themselves. This does not mean that teachers take a laissez-faire point of view about students and their behaviors. Students do not just do what they want to do; quite the contrary.

To encourage self-regulation and self-management requires extensive interactions between teachers and children and among children. Teachers must create conditions in support of such interactions. For example, Linda and Delia, who work with different age groups—one an older and the other a younger group—have created ways for students to address and solve together the conflicts that arise between and among students. Each uses some form of group or class meeting to discuss interpersonal issues, identify problems, and develop solutions to these problems. Children receive ideas and suggestions from their peers about what they can do differently, and later they receive feedback about how they have done.

Delia also has provided an example of how she views and works with a child who, in the past at Ochoa and in other schools, would be excluded from the class and perhaps placed in a special education setting. She describes the child in quite graphic terms with regard to what he says and does in her classroom. She doesn't like what he does and has sought ways to assist Manuel in altering how he interacts in his classroom and, more important, how he develops more productive ways of being a child.

Delia, Linda, Laura, and Sue have each noted a critical dimension to resolving student behavior issues. They each have expressed the importance of offering all students schoolwork that engages them and challenges their minds. In addition, providing choices for students on what they will investigate and learn seems to mitigate what in the past were issues related to student misbehavior.

All of the teachers have alluded to ideas discussed in the introduction that have made sense to them. Addressing each person's beliefs about control played an important part in what and how they rethought ways of addressing behavior in class and school. Although teachers urged students to regulate themselves, caring and compassion played a major role in developing various activities and strategies for reducing what used to be a major issue at Ochoa—student misbehavior.

Sue nicely suggests the importance that her colleagues and principal have played in encouraging her to address issues of student behavior in ways uncommon to what she used to do. Several other writers alluded to these important support structures for themselves. Hence, student behavior cannot be productively addressed in isolation from other aspects of schooling, including the work of students and support from teacher colleagues, who can discuss and examine with each other ideas, such as caring and compassion, control, and the importance of engaging student work. These ideas suggest new activities and strategies for mitigating typical student misbehavior.

8

Developing Creativity Through Indigenous Invention

The ECC Project assumes that teachers at Ochoa and elsewhere have the intellect to create—as well as implement—innovations in schooling; all innovations need not come through state or federal legislation or edicts of the school district. Indigenous invention breaks the bondage of top-to-bottom management of school practices, structures, and curricula. Teachers, the principal, students, and parents are offered an opportunity to create the school changes that they deem necessary. Their voices are meaningful in meeting the educational needs that are applicable to the particular circumstances of the children, their families, and the socioeconomic status of their neighborhoods. Teachers at Ochoa have begun to unleash their creativity and are encouraging their students to do likewise.

In the first chapter, we talked about indigenous invention, which encourages teachers, principals, parents and other community members, as well as students, to make decisions and recreate all schooling structures, activities, and practices that existed in the past. It also encourages the invention of curricula and practices that are in the context of students' real lives. Such indigenous inventions appear to work better in schools (and communities) than do practices and structures that are created outside by state or federal legislation or district edict. Furthermore, we believe these inventions are more likely to be accepted and implemented inside the schools and communities than those that are created by outsiders.

Certainly, indigenous invention places the responsibility of creativity on the involved adults, but in addition, the new activities that emanate from this process also promote the creativity of the children. The importance of local people—those who are indigenous to a school and its neighborhood—seeing themselves as inventors/creators provides the platform for launching educational reform and for achieving the purposes of the ECC Project. The adults and children of a local school and neighborhood become inventors.

In order for indigenous invention to flourish, my colleagues at the school and I sought the creation of a set of conditions in the school to promote its development. There were certain assumptions that guided and continue to guide the process of indigenous invention at Ochoa:

1. Continuation of standard practices and standard results will hamper—not promote—invention, and no one practice or idea will be sufficient for all children to learn the important knowledge and skills necessary in a postindustrial democratic society.
2. Standard ways of looking at children and how they learn must be examined and new work created that promotes nonstandard ways for students to think and be.
3. The work of teachers shifts to include creative or inventive tasks, which require heavy doses of thinking, rather than just acting, and such mental work will greatly contribute to change in schools.
4. The more varied schooling ideas and practices are and the more they promote variety in student thinking and knowing, the more benefits will be derived by children.
5. All individuals have a great capacity to invent, not just a few chosen individuals whose roles are to create.
6. Given the fact that indigenous invention requires human judgment that is rooted in agreed-upon criteria for judging

the worth and quality of inventions, it takes advantage of this judgment and encourages variety, rather than traditional ways of thinking and standard operating procedures.

7. Creating the conditions for indigenous invention promotes the capacities of teachers to continuously reinvent what they think and do as circumstances change at the school and they examine their new knowledge.

The invention process at Ochoa began with an examination of present educational circumstances in the school, after-school, and larger community context. In dialogue sessions, we examined the ideas and beliefs that were the basis for the existing practices and structures. Then we searched (and continue to search) for new or alternative ideas and concepts from inside as well as outside the community. Based on our findings, new practices and structures are being created. Local parents, teachers, principals, and children are using their own knowledge to examine and alter what existed. The results include many of the changes discussed in earlier chapters.

Indigenous invention attempts to overcome the shortcomings found in many school reform projects. Two words appear in most of those school change efforts: innovation and implementation. The designers of those projects create the innovations that are to replace the old teaching practices and school structures, and then they have to develop a way for school faculties to put the innovations into practice. That's where the teachers and principals enter the picture, because they are the ones who must implement in the schools and classrooms the innovations that have been designed for them.

It is true that experience and research have improved the process of implementation of innovation in school change efforts. For example: (a) Opportunities are sometimes offered for teachers to mutually adapt and/or alter the innovations, and (b) designers of the innovations provide concrete and specific features of the agreed-upon innovations, furnish opportunities for teachers to try out the innovations, and coach the teachers in the use of the innovations in their classrooms. However, even this enlightened view suggests a less than positive picture for changing schools, let alone encouraging a fundamental and systemic restructuring of education nationwide. The difficulty arises because of the basic views of teachers that are inherent in a school's culture. When innovations to be implemented stray too far from the "regularities" and culture of the school, teachers reject them as impractical and too idealistic. J. I. Goodlad and M. K. Klein (1974) found that although principals and teachers *reported* using reform-oriented curricular guides and materials, they rarely did so in practice. Instead, they continued to maintain their own one-way communications with the students.

Another flaw exists in the implementation of innovations concept: Particular practices and activities that work and make sense in one place may have serious difficulties in other settings. When reformers take an effective practice from one school and urge teachers from another to implement the practice, the chances of the same effectiveness prevailing in the new school decline dramatically. In other words, the effectiveness of one set of innovations in a single place does not generalize to other settings.

In 1990, when the ECC Project began its efforts at Ochoa, an indigenous invention strategy seemed not only theoretically but also practically more feasible than an implementation of innovation strategy. We did not know, however, what particular conditions inside and outside the school would encourage and promote invention. The overall question guiding the project was "Can it be done?" Certainly, at times during the past 5 years the answer appeared to be "No," but then a resounding "Yes" would encourage all of us to proceed as planned—or more accurately, as unplanned. The question of "Can it be done?" continues today.

During dialogue sessions, we began by contrasting implementation of innovations strategy with indigenous invention. These contrasts hinted at some conditions that we would establish to begin the project. One idea focused on organizational design and the role of human beings in that organization. In Chapter 1, it was stated that existing design features of traditional schooling (the graded school structure, for example) evolved out of the conventional 19th-century industrial manufacturing model. The implementation of innovation strategy also has features related to that Industrial Age model. For example, a group of researchers creates a school innovation (the design) and the process for implementation (manufacturing process). In turn, the organization (school district or other governing body) communicates the process to the teachers and principals (workers on the production line). It is up to them to make the newly designed products (the students).

One question that inevitably comes forth in such a concept is, "Who has the ability/intelligence to create/invent?" In the standard view of intelligence, only a small percentage of the population has the supposed intelligence to create and invent, and because manufacturing requires so many workers to make the products, employers often assume that the line workers have only average to below-average levels of intelligence and cannot think for themselves or create what and how they will manufacture products.

A similar ideology prevails in modern-day schooling. School districts, in conjunction with university faculty, have developed specialists who create policies and innovations, including curriculum designs and materials for implementation. Teachers don't create the designs or materials; they implement the designs and use the materials specified by others. Furthermore, school districts have created staff development offices and activities, where teachers go and are expected to learn about what they should do. These ideas have their foundation built on the old ideas of who has the intelligence to create. These designers, researchers, and administrators must assume that teachers cannot think for themselves and create what and how they will educate children. Just as the assembly-line workers are excluded from the creative process, teachers do not have the opportunity to invent.

The foundation for indigenous invention develops by first rejecting or turning upside down the old ideas about organizations and individuals. Particular persons (whose intellect may or may not be as high or higher than others) are not placed in exclusive roles as creators or designers. Instead, the project seeks development of conditions in which anyone and everyone in the school who wants to invent may do so. This concept is encouraged among the children as well as the adults. Children are encouraged to create, not to replicate someone else's knowledge in their heads and in action. They are encouraged by teachers, and often parents, to create their own knowledge through projects they develop and undertake with their teachers and peers.

SUE: Without textbooks and prescribed work sheets, an important part of schooling involves community resources, the utilization of which is part of indigenous invention. Moving students away from their classroom, making them aware and a part of the larger community helps them see themselves connected to the world in new ways. During one study project, we invited four or five researchers and graduate students at the University of

Arizona to come to the classroom and be involved with the
students in our project work. Also, students from the Hispanic
fraternity volunteer to come into our classroom twice a week to
work with our students. During the summer and on weekends,
our students have been involved with programs such as Native
Images, Nuevos Horizontes, the Audubon Society, and other
nature-focused organizations. Now, during the fifth year, with
school budgets being tight, our classes are only allowed to share
one field trip a year, so Laura and I have begun to utilize the city
bus system to get the kids into the community and more aware
and involved with real life outside their neighborhood.

LAURA: The place I find most of my inventions is with the students
themselves. In class meetings we discuss what they are interested in and how to pursue it. I haven't let go of everything I
believed with regard to how to learn; I frequently develop strategies in those areas. However, most often now, I let the students
choose what we're going to study and how they are going to
pursue their studies. I present alternatives to the usual ways, or
the students may suggest alternatives.

Sue and I developed plays with the students for several years.
The fourth year of the ECC Project was a milestone for us,
because not only did the students decide to have a play, but they
also wrote it, decided upon songs for it, made costumes, did the
lighting, played the synthesizer, and did most of the directing.
The students created and developed an extraordinary play. They
also chose the facets of the play in which they would be involved.
It was an extremely difficult time for Sue and me, because the
most important things we learned were how to keep our mouths
shut and our hands off. It was an all-student effort.

More recently, the students and I spent 6 weeks investigating
chocolate. We created text sets for reading (e.g., "Chocolate
Fever"), math problems, an exceptional amount of research and
writing, and more thinking skills than I could have imagined.
Mars Candy Company announced that it was going to introduce
a new color of M&Ms, so my students polled the student body
about which color they preferred: blue, purple, or pink. Then they
wrote letters to the Mars Company, explaining what we had been
doing and what they had learned. When we received responses
to our letters, the students were ecstatic. They not only recog-

nized a real purpose for their letters and were rewarded for their efforts with individual letters and information, but they also received coupons for free candy. For most of my students, it was the first time they had ever had anything addressed specifically to them. Several even announced that they were going to write back.

Part of every one of our study units are the students' reactions or evaluations. Several reactions to the chocolate study were virtually unanimous: "This was fun!" "I'm tired of thinking. Can't we do something easier?" and "I'm sick of chocolate!" Sometimes these are measures of success in my room.

Developing choices in the classroom has meant that the students were choosing not only how they would apply themselves to learning, but also how to do it independently of me. This does not mean that they avoided any aspect of learning. I still believe that students must be able to read, write, and figure out problems. Developing choice and still expecting development of necessary skills is the most difficult aspect of my involvement in the ECC Project.

ANA: One thing I've come to expect is that when children really get into their creative mode, they're either very quiet or they're very noisy. My teammate, Delia, has a special skill whereby she can filter in what she wants to hear and the noise level is not as distracting to her. On one particular afternoon the noise level seemed far less bothersome to me, because each student was eager to be heard, to share his or her ideas. Interest, enthusiasm, and motivation were evident as every child was participating.

The challenge was to make the study units more real to the students, so they were asked to suggest what they could do to make that happen. The 6- and 7-year-olds began suggesting topics or places that were of interest to them, and ultimately they divided into groups according to their special interests. The interest groups included a doctor's office, a grocery store, police officers, insects, pizza, and construction.

The children in my homeroom class had their learning logs accessible, and because they were scattered among the study groups, we suggested that they record the ideas of the group. Delia and I took this time to sit and "kid watch"—as well as "kid listen." We observed that one girl took a leadership role in the small planning group, but chose not to participate when it came time to make a presentation to the whole class.

As each group made its presentation, the rest of the class offered suggestions and questioned some of the planning. For example, they wanted to know why there weren't any nurses in the doctor's office.

As the class ended we felt that we, as teachers, had freely exhibited indigenous invention, with the students suggesting the curriculum. The students had exhibited and recorded some of their existing knowledge and provided a foundation upon which we can build future studies that will include reading, writing, mathematics, science, and various other subject fields.

SUE: When it comes to creating ideas for a classroom, I think I'm my own worst enemy. My problem is not having too few ideas, it's having so many that I'm frustrated when there is no time to pursue them. I feel I'm a jack-of-all-trades, master-of-none type of person. I'm interested in a lot of different things. I play the guitar and piano a little; I've been an arts and crafts teacher (but definitely am not an artist), and I've been a reading specialist (and in my second life would become a librarian). Because of my relationship with the Title 1 math and science project, I've become really curious about how numbers work and why things act the way they do. My mind just seems to pick up on an idea and begin webbing further and further afield. Taming all of this into some workable (teachable) whole has always been challenging, but fun.

What I'm beginning to realize now is that children have the same kinds of eager curiosity about their world. When I do all the planning, I'm not only taking away some of their native curiosity, but also actually robbing them of a chance to create, develop, and pursue their own ideas and interests. I do believe it is the teacher's responsibility to create an environment that will stimulate children to be curious about their world. They can't be curious and want to explore new ideas in a vacuum. As I think back, the insect inquiry unit [see Chapters 6 and 10] was partially successful because children were first given "wonder and wander" time—a time to interact with the fascinating little creatures we call insects. In between the periods of exploration was time to provide background information they could use to describe what they were seeing, and time to ask questions and do their own investigations. I don't feel kids have to discover everything for themselves any more than teachers should have to reinvent school without taking into consideration thoughts and ideas of others who are exploring similar issues.

One part of helping children be creative may be providing engaging environments that will stimulate their natural curiosity. Another may be honoring their right to ask questions and learn in their own ways, rather than insisting they follow our ways of learning. A third, I believe, may be valuing their early efforts. I think of when babies utter their first words or take their first steps, adults cheer and applaud and encourage, but when children start to read or write, we say, "No, no, no. Do it this way!" When I was 7, my grandmother wanted to teach me to sew. By the time I had taken my first zipper out seven times, I hated sewing and vowed never to sew again. When I was 12, my 15-year-old cousin said, "Come on, let's make a skirt." We bought the material, I put it together and wore it throughout high school. I've been a seamstress ever since. (This also may be an example of children learning from each other, rather than from an adult.)

ANA: My 6- and 7-year-old students were busy with math manipulatives when two girls invited me over to show me a game they had created. It was a very intricate game and it gave me the idea to entice the children to become inventors of math games. My original idea was to have the children sit in a circle while I taught them a math game; that was something we had done successfully in the past. But it occurred to me that the students could expand on problem-solving/thinking processes if they created their own games.

Some children chose to work independently, others as partners or a group of three, and after about 40 minutes of creating and inventing games, we all sat down to share our results. Various math strands were represented in their creations.

The first to demonstrate were the two girls who had earlier shown me the game they invented. It was complex, yet simple, and included using a number dial and dice to create an addition problem. Then they counted out playing cards to represent the total. The player with the most cards at the end of the game was the winner (number sense and probability math strand).

One girl demonstrated a game doing a graph, pulling out letters and filling in the spaces (number sense using a graph). A team of three students showed us how to make pictures from the relation-shapes. We counted how many different shapes there were on each child's picture (number sense and geometry math strand). All the boys made designs on the geoboards. We all guessed what shapes we could see in their designs (geometry math strand).

One girl exercised her independence and chose to work as a scientist rather than a mathematician. She put a leaf in a small container of water and shook it to make bubbles. She was hypothesizing that the leaf caused the bubbles in the water (energy and patterns of change in science strands).

The hour flowed smoothly. The children were engaged in their own inventions as well as those of the other children. Young minds can be very creative when they aren't contained by rigorous disciplines.

Reflections

One thing that is prevalent throughout the teachers' stories about creativity and indigenous invention is the unleashing of thoughts and actions in the classroom. Prescribed curriculum, practices, and structures of the past are viewed as a vacuum in which creativity is restrained.

Now separated from practices and curricula designed by others, teachers and students find themselves free to wonder about and explore as they see fit the real things in their own real world. Teachers are both reaching out and reaching in. They are reaching out to resources of interesting knowledge and expertise in the neighborhood and larger community; they are reaching in to ideas and beliefs that they and the children maintain.

In Ochoa classrooms, the amount of creativity and curiosity that children are revealing is often sufficient to provide units of study in which the children have a sense of ownership. This sense of ownership promotes engagement of their minds and further extension of their own creative abilities. More and more, teachers and students are realizing their abilities to create and do for themselves, rather than relying on others who in the past had the responsibility for telling them what they must teach or learn—about topics that often may not be relevant to their lives today or in their future lives as citizens of the larger community.

Also, as the designers and implementers of their own curriculum and teaching practices, teachers are gaining knowledge to better evaluate the worthiness and applicability of work created by those who have historically been authorized to design their education system.

Reference

Goodlad, J. I., & Klein, M. K. (1974). *Looking behind the classroom door.* Worthington, OH: Charles A. Jones.

9

Assessing Student Achievement

Alternative education requires alternative means for assessing student achievement. There was consensus among Ochoa teachers that traditional norm-referenced testing had never been appropriate for the children at Ochoa, and these standardized tests definitely could not adequately reflect the learning acquired by the students in the alternative teaching environment that the teachers were promoting. As teachers became more and more involved in alternative teaching practices and school structures, they began to create and develop their own guidelines for assessing the results of their practices.

When the ECC Project began, scores on norm-referenced tests placed Ochoa students at the bottom of the lowest quartile of school scores in the district. The school and district had mounted efforts to improve scores by bringing in special programs for the lowest scoring children, and teachers provided instruction focused on basic skills. Yet, none of the efforts ameliorated the scores. Ochoa children were viewed by the district, community, and the teachers as underachieving at best; at worst, the view persisted that these children could not achieve, especially in a manner equivalent to those children who were often referred to as middle-class.

Dialogue sessions often focused on the lack of student achievement, and discussion usually led to the traditional testing measures that supported this negative view of Ochoa children. In dialogue sessions, teachers then began to seek understanding of norm-referenced tests and the knowledge and skills they assessed. The assumption was made that these testing measures and the knowledge and skills reflected in them required reinvention.

Discussion about educational reform often centers on the structures and methods of educating children, and little attention is given to recreating the knowledge and skills promoted in schooling. The ECC Project saw the importance of attending to both, based on the belief that certain methods of teaching advance particular knowledge and skills. If one is altered, then the other must be altered. For example, if the methods of teaching reading are recast, then a new set of knowledge and skills will be necessary to promote literacy.

Old knowledge and skills may contribute as much to poor children not achieving as the educational methods used. For instance, syllabification appears on most norm-referenced tests as an important reading skill, and teachers provide classroom activities for learning syllabification. If such a skill is essential for learning to read, then it makes sense to develop new methods to learn this skill. On the other hand, despite the fact that items related to syllabification appear on norm-referenced tests, and districts often list it in curriculum guides, if syllabification does *not* promote literacy, then the time and effort devoted to it can interfere with children's acquiring the knowledge and skills that are essential to literacy.

Some believe that changes in assessment activities will directly alter curriculum and classroom instruction, causing new knowledge and skills to be acquired. However, as reviewed in this chapter, Ochoa teachers came to view assessment and curriculum as related phenomena. They occur together and mutually encourage each other; what is assessed is what is promoted, and what is promoted must be assessed.

Another aspect of assessment has to do with the public's often negative view of public education, especially the education offered to poor children of color. This distrust in the adequacy of public schools appears to stem from results of the present system, including such things as scores on norm-referenced tests and school dropout rates. As the importance of public education wanes in the minds of the public, material and rhetorical support for public schooling wanes; therefore, one must wonder what will happen to poor children of color if the public system ceases to serve this population.

As discussed in earlier chapters, the ECC Project promoted the belief that these children had and could learn essential knowledge and skills if the old and traditional methods of teaching could be reinvented to better serve the particular characteristics of the student enrollment and the social, economic, and political circumstances of these children in today's world. By the third year of the project, my colleagues and I were aware that many school structures and teaching practices had changed. Because that confidence existed, teachers and project staff began to explicitly discuss strategies for changing ways of assessing the school and its programs to more adequately reflect what children are learning in Ochoa classrooms.

One of the first and necessary steps in our assessment strategy was to seek a waiver for Ochoa from the district's required norm-referenced testing and the existing district curriculum guidelines. The district granted the waiver, accepting instead of these tests the use of a new state assessment activity called the Arizona State Assessment Plan (ASAP). This effort was finalized at the beginning of the fifth year of the project; meanwhile, however, teachers had been focusing explicit attention to the development of an alternative assessment system that would be applicable to the new practices and structures that were evolving at Ochoa School.

At this time, their assessment processes focus on the following:

1. Promoting the value of human judgments—by teachers and parents and other members of the community—about the worth of a child's performance and the products and productions of children's schoolwork. As students engage in contextualized learning activities, they are studying and investigating real things and events in order to make changes in real things, when possible. As a result of these studies, students have discernible performances by which they can show how they thought about a set of circumstances, identified a problem, and developed a solution in their productions or products.
2. Advancing judgments about the worth of what children *say* they know in relation to the schoolwork they have done. This

focuses on the production and products of the children as well
and includes what the children say they know and thought
about as they perform and do the action. Teachers and others
judge the worth of this stated knowledge and thinking in
relation to the children's actions (products and productions).

An aspect of the project's assessment strategy that is being developed has to do with examination of student achievement during
the second, third, and fourth years of the project, when standardized
or norm-referenced tests were administered.

It can be noted at this time that since the project began, the
scores of Ochoa students on district or state-imposed tests have
improved in several areas. During the third and fourth years of the
project, English-speaking Ochoa students scored above the district
averages in mathematics and writing on the Arizona Student Assessment Plan, and scores in writing were among the highest in the
district.

Much more examination and understanding of student achievement remains; however, on the face of the issue, norm-referenced
achievement scores are higher than they were 5 years ago and the
responses on more authentic assessment measures show above-
average attainment of the students.

All of this provides a backdrop to what the teachers will highlight
in this chapter. As their involvement in project work deepened, their
commitments to alternative forms of assessment grew stronger.

ANA: My beliefs on standardized tests have never been favorable;
the results don't tell what a child knows—only what can be memorized and later forgotten. Also, the content is usually culturally
biased.

It both saddens and angers me that school districts across the
country still fall prey to the million-dollar testing industry that
uses archaic methods of testing at the expense of our children.
We need to stop comparing children and pitting one against the
other. Let us instead closely examine how we are preparing students for the real world. Does the child understand and communicate with confidence his or her knowledge and skills? Is the
child able to problem solve, self-regulate, and become an independent learner?

Report cards in the traditional sense do not suffice, because they sort and label children. We need to recognize students for what they can do, not what they cannot do.

At Ochoa we are in a transition period of moving away from report cards to developing ways in which to document how children learn through their questioning, discovering, communicating, problem solving, and self-evaluation. This is not an easy task, but we are continuing in this struggle.

My views on assessment have taken an alternate direction. I find I am becoming more aware of what I do and why. It takes constant effort to let the children do it, rather than giving them the answers. I'm discovering the importance of reading circumstances: Was I too controlling? Did I talk too much?

As soon as the school day is over, I sit down at the computer and reflect on how the day went. I may include all of the observations that were significant to me, questions or comments I might have, as well as the comments of students, other teachers, and parents. This information becomes part of the students' portfolios. It helps validate what the child can do and what he or she has learned.

I remember Delia, my teammate, was asked during a dialogue session why children's comments were important to write down. She answered something to the effect that the written comments help her assess children and help children assess themselves, and they also help parents see their children's growth. This process has become an important communication and assessment tool for us. It demonstrates the thinking process of the child and the language being used, which is important to document in a bilingual setting.

BECKY: I am very interested in assessment and am conducting research in the use of portfolios as an alternative to traditional testing practices. Children at our school generally do not score very high on the standardized tests that our state demands. I believe these scores are not very accurate: They do not show what our children know, they do not show their growth as learners, and they sort out children as losers. The portfolios are a collection of student work that shows what they've done from the beginning to the end of the school year.

In each portfolio is a wealth of information about each child's individual growth and his or her weakness and strength in language arts. However, possibly what is more important is that these children are learning about themselves as learners and have gained a great amount of confidence in themselves. The children know what makes them good writers and they have a goal they can reach. Many of the children are excited about their portfolios and are writing more than ever before.

Portfolios require a lot of work, but the benefits seem to outweigh that extra work. I'm very pleased so far with what I've seen and learned through using them.

MARIANNE: Assessing student achievement used to mean administering a test in English that was standardized throughout the district. Questions on the test were often culturally biased, and it didn't matter if the student's dominant language was English, Spanish—or Vietnamese. Interim assessment would be answering questions at the end of a story in the students' reader or a test at the end of a study unit to see how much information the student had retained from the textbook on math, social studies, or science. Standardized tests were also used to label students for special education classes, with the overall score determining the placement.

Becky and I have been assessing our students' writing through the use of portfolios; each month we collect two or three samples of each student's writing. Initially, we posed the following questions to our students: What makes a good writer? Why is this a good story? Did you like the story? Why or why not? The students' answers became the criteria we've been using to assess their writing. Those answers included: "It's interesting and you want to read more." "Good choice of words." "It makes you picture the story in your head." "It has a beginning, middle, and end." "It has lots of details." "You can connect it to your own life experiences or feelings."

We also came up with a checklist of what we call observable writing behaviors, that is, interaction and collaboration with others, letter formation, interest, pencil grip, strategies used for spelling, revising, risk taking, and editing. We feel the purpose of the writing portfolio is to demonstrate evidence of growth over time. It reveals how the writing process has developed as well as the product. It allows students to take an active role in becoming responsible and accountable for their learning. It provides a good picture of what the child is doing and where the child is going. It's almost as if you can see the child's thinking.

I feel we've come a long way, because today assessment means looking at each individual child in a nonthreatening way; it's a daily process that is ongoing, no matter what the child is doing. Still, we have a lot of questions: What do we do with this information? Who's going to look at the portfolios? How many pieces should be included in each portfolio, and who should select them?

ANA: With all due respect, we call the observation of children "kid watching." This is a valuable source of assessment, but it goes beyond the constructs of observing the child. It is knowing that the child knows.

I was conferring with one of my 6-year-old girls regarding a graph she had made with relation-shapes. She had been asked to make a representation, compare, and write about it. I was having difficulty understanding her inventive writing. The letter sound symbols did not match some of the words, so I asked her to read it to me. I still did not understand her explanation, but I knew that she knew because of the confidence she demonstrated and her perseverance in explaining it over and over until—finally—I got it. She had started the graph representation from the right, classifying "less" by gradually moving toward the left with "more." Of course it made sense, if I looked at the graph through her eyes and ignored my perceived notion of how it should look.

Every day I learn more through the children's eyes, and in this special world there are no adults labeling them right or wrong. Children just know.

LAURA: A number of times I've been weak-kneed about what I was doing. I'd think "Maybe this isn't good. I don't know how to evaluate what I'm doing." I had a lot of "What if . . . " questions. What if next year, when the students are in middle school, they get clobbered by the traditional system? I think we all feel a responsibility for that. I don't want my kids to move to another school and be devastated by the traditional system, with teachers saying they're stupid and don't understand things—or asking why they don't know how to divide or where to put quotation marks in a sentence. I don't want the child to think I have failed him or her because I didn't insist that multiplication tables be memorized.

But on the other hand, I don't know how to "make" children learn anything. I know how resistant they used to become—almost hostile—to the idea that they would have to memorize something. They resisted the memorization process because they couldn't comprehend the value of what they were attempting to learn. But if my students have problems later, I don't want them to feel that I've failed them.

Part of the worry goes back to how we can get other people to value the process that we're in at Ochoa and to allow teachers at other schools to begin to develop their own types of things. If the educational system continues to give such high priority to standardized test scores, then we're going to continue to run into this dilemma. I know what we're doing is really important and I believe in it, but I worry about the children in their future years when they must face traditional teaching practices and testing.

SUE: Meetings were held at the end of the project's fourth school year and during the summer to look at the ways we were assessing children and how this fit with the new curriculum we were trying to create in the classroom. We were asking such questions as "What is assessment?" "What kinds of assessments have we been using to evaluate the new work of students and teachers?" "Does the kind of assessment we've been using really support our new curriculum?"

We then returned to our classrooms to explore our ideas with students in the classroom, to document these ideas and bring them back to share with others. It was at this point that I found several teams really involved in working on assessment tools to help measure what students were doing.

One day, with the help of Title 1 funds, Laura and I met with Delia, Chris, and ECC Project staffer Anna Loebe to share what we had come up with. This proved to be a time that changed my ideas about assessment. By looking at children's work, they had begun to look at documenting the program or curriculum and assessing how well it met the needs of students, teachers, and parents. From that time, Laura and I began developing and trying various tools, such as portfolios, student self-evaluations, and the like.

DELIA: I feel that many children's lives have been ruined by test results and their negative impact. Identical tests, which are insensitive to language dominance or culture or experiential knowledge, are administered to all children. To me, these standardized tests, which teachers are mandated to administer, represent worthless statistics to everybody except the school districts. They, no doubt, frantically compare test scores of each school in the district to see which school scores at the bottom and which at the top. Unfortunately, in the past we at Ochoa were more likely to be near the bottom than the top, because the same tests were used for all children, regardless of language dominance or culture. Principals in some schools sometimes use upcoming tests as a scare tactic for teachers. "The school's image is at stake" is the implied message. The threat of damaging the school's image produces the practice of teachers "teaching to the test," although the tests generally have nothing or very little to do with experiential knowledge. Ultimately, the teacher has the unpleasant task of announcing any negative results to the child and/or parent.

The foremost concern of parents seems to be how their child compares to other children, and these tests are supposed to provide that comparison. The message is that every student has the very same brain, background, body, ambition, talent, and life, so the same test would do for everybody. It's amazing to me that children by the age of 6 demonstrate test anxiety. I'll never forget the experience of seeing two children vomit as we discussed a standardized test I was going to administer. Test phobia that many adults experience obviously begins at a very early age in life.

Today, assessment has taken on a different meaning—a more friendly, child-teacher-parent meaning. Instead of definite dates being set for testing, assessment is an ongoing, daily monitoring, and the child takes an active part in it. Ana, my teammate, says, "Children can now use assessment to raise their levels of awareness and develop thinking processes and dispositions." They can identify their own weaknesses and develop strengths based on their internal sense of responsibility. Assessing and monitoring ourselves is a natural process in our classroom, because children are asked to reflect daily on their work. They analyze, interpret, and record their findings in their dominant language. It's an individualized process, and there is no comparison of one to the other. In regular dialogue with the students, teachers and students become a community of learners; we help each other understand strengths and weaknesses in a positive way.

Ana points out that children are not learning the teacher's value system, as they did in a traditional classroom. In the past, parents would come to the classrooms for various activities in which the teacher would attempt to show them what they had taught and what their children had learned. It was always a stressful 2-hour meeting, with the teacher trying to answer the parents' questions about the progress of their child. The teacher was always "on stage" as parents attempted to assess their work and the progress of the child. This year at a gathering of parents it was very different. The *children* explained the school environment and the student work to the parents.

LAURA: I certainly knew what I was doing when I had a grade book. I filled it each year with all my knowledge of what each child had learned. I haven't the vaguest idea what it means now. I worry about the kids who were relegated, as Charlie Brown once said, to "Straight Blah Students." They must have been so much more than that, but these little (anonymous) children had nothing but Bs and Cs in my grade book. That dictated who they were and what they had accomplished according to my textbooks.

I not only know my students better now, but I also remember them better. Having developed something new to do in the classroom in some ways meant my becoming a different person. Change is not possible in only one dimension.

During the past 5 years we've looked for and invented a variety of ways to assess our students' progress. Just as important, however, has been the development of ways to evaluate our teaching program. I feel the need to look at objectives and goals and know that what I'm inventing is meeting the needs of the students. I need to know that I'm not hurting or limiting their educations. We have developed several different instruments, such as portfolios and student self-evaluations, for tracking the skills and objectives of both the students and ourselves.

Assessment cannot be tacked onto the end of a project. It is an integral part of teaching. It's very time-consuming to try to do assessment and create curricula all at once. In fact, without assistance, I believe it's impossible. I need the expertise and advice of teachers who are bilingual, for example, to make sure that I am not only supporting their learning in English but also encouraging their learning in Spanish. I also seek student input. It is just as essential as determining what and how we're learning.

LINDA: The fact that traditional testing practices are not helpful to students, teachers, or parents is reason enough for me to seek alternatives. I shared my questions, thoughts, and beliefs about assessment with other teachers. We talked about different ways to show what a child (or adult) knows. We came up with a variety of alternatives, but always in the end I still had to put a grade on a report card. We proceeded to talk about what grades mean and the criteria for grades. We began to seek additional evaluations—not just mine as the teacher. We asked students to evaluate each other as well as themselves in mindful ways. I had conversations with each student when it came time to do report cards and we both agreed on the grade that went on the card. I feel that in the first 4 years of the ECC Project assessment is the area in which the least amount of progress was made, but efforts in alternative assessment stepped up considerably during the fifth year, and more effort in that area is to come.

SUE: I wanted to get away from the idea of grades. Everyone has a different meaning for the letter "A." To one, it means the students have mastered a certain skill or acquired certain knowledge that the teacher has deemed important. To another, it means a student has made an outstanding effort. To still others, it shows the degree of change over time. To parents, it has still other connotations. What I wanted to do was to describe, to paint a picture of each child so that he or she, the parents, and I would be able to "see" that child and what he or she was able to do. I wanted children to see that they were growing in knowledge and skills.

I decided one way was to have the children in the intermediate classes set their own evaluation criteria for various projects. In one unit, they chose a set of books (one on the human body, another on the ocean floor, etc.) to read and then share what they had learned with others in the class. Before the presentations, we talked about what would make a good presentation and recorded their answers on the board. During each group's presentation, the other students recorded what they liked about the presentation, what they learned, and suggestions for making it better the next time. These evaluations were shared orally and in writing after each presentation. Each group also evaluated its own work against the criteria it had set for itself. This seemed to be a positive learning experience for the children.

Laura and I began to talk about how we could get a feeling for how the children viewed their classroom experiences. We began by asking students to rate themselves, from one to five, on each topic we had explored during the week. Then we asked them to say what they really liked and really disliked and to suggest something they would like to do differently. This became a real source of feedback for us. We learned, for example, that during phys. ed., boys would really like to be involved in football, so we made that an option during that class period. One young man said: "I want to do more arithmetic." I asked what he meant. Pointing to the division sign on the calculator, he said, "I want to learn how to do this." I showed him work we had been doing that involved division, but somehow I had not labeled it for him. I am collecting these feedback sheets and starting to build a picture of all the students, what they perceive as their strengths, weaknesses, likes, and dislikes, and so on.

As the semester has gone on, we have moved into unit or project evaluations, which are another way of helping children see what they have learned. When report card time came for the first 9 weeks, Laura and I created an overview of the quarter and asked each child to do the same. I was amazed at their insights about their own learning and how similar their evaluations were to my own. In fact, many times during our one-on-one conferences with the students, we were able to point out and support strengths that they were unsure they possessed.

CHRIS: The issue of assessment is clearly a complex one. Several teachers and I had been considering the issue, not only during dialogue sessions but also as part of ongoing mathematics workshops provided by the Title 1 project. We had concluded that assessing the children is only a part of our task.

We can never truly know what the children know, but we *can* demonstrate the quality of what we are offering children. We can document that we are providing children with rich opportunities to think and reason, to construct their own understandings about the world around them. We can prove that our children have had programs that are valued by educators nationally. With this in mind, Delia Hakim, Ana Andrade, other members of the first-grade team, and I created what we call a "program portfolio."

It was a difficult but exciting process. We began by putting our philosophy into print. We listed the guiding principles that we used to make decisions during the year. Included in our list were our hopes: (a) to develop the natural curiosity of children, (b) to have the children reflect on their theories, (c) to be teachers who facilitate rather than control, (d) to connect in meaningful ways with parents and the community, and (e) to have children think about real problems to make a real difference in their world. Because we were looking at mathematics in particular at that time, our philosophy section also included documents from the National Council of Teachers of Mathematics (NCTM) that support our beliefs. Among these documents was a list titled "What Industry Expects of New Employees" and "A Summary of Changes in Content and Emphasis in K-4 Mathematics." Each page was written in both English and Spanish. These pages would be useful to explain our beliefs to any interested party: parents, administrators, other teachers, or members of the community.

The other sections of the portfolio were to provide documentation about how we were helping three groups (parents, children, and ourselves as teachers) have access to learning about quality mathematics.

As we created the section about access for parents, we realized that we had provided many, many chances for parents to learn about the kind of mathematics required in the world today. It felt very rewarding to gather copies of newsletters that we had sent home to parents that year. We included agendas, sign-in sheets, and parent comments about the Family Math nights we'd had, and informal parent dialogues [see *cafecitos* in Chapter 10, this volume] that we had conducted. We listed the ways we had included parents' expertise in their children's learning at school. We also listed bulletin board displays that had informed parents what was going on in the classroom.

The section on access for children had three parts. First, we listed each activity that supported learning in mathematics in which the children had participated. Then we correlated those activities with the different strands of mathematics, to get an overall look at the children's experiences. Again, it was very rewarding to see how the activities included measurement, probability and statistics, geometry, number, logical thinking, and pattern.

The second way we documented access for children was by providing evidence that the activities were sufficiently rich to allow access to children with varying amounts of experience. We took several activities and created a checklist to note the strengths that each child showed, what strategies each child had used, and significant aspects of each child's work.

The third way that we demonstrated that our children had rich opportunities was by including copies of complimentary notes handwritten by visitors to our classroom.

The final section of our program portfolio described access for us teachers, as learners. Just as people feel good about a physician keeping up with his or her field, parents, administrators, and members of the community need to know that we teachers also continue to have chances to learn. We listed the workshops we had attended that year, the dialogue sessions and topics in which we had participated, the classes we had taken, articles we had read that were important to us, and a published journal article that we had written.

It took many days to compile our program portfolio, yet we learned a lot from this overview of a year with a group of children. We felt extremely professional as we worked. We felt validated; we *had* provided children with important experiences. We compiled evidence, which in past years might have disappeared into the wind. We hoped that this program portfolio would provide the basis for future years' portfolios, that the philosophy section could merely be updated and that the other three sections could use similar formats.

I believe that educators traditionally spend a tremendous amount of time testing children, almost dissecting them in their anxiety to show that children are making progress. There is a negative impact on children. It reminds me of pulling up a seed-ling every month to measure the roots to see if it is growing. I'm thinking a lot these days about the value of shifting the burden of proof to teachers. I would prefer that we put ourselves to the test.

SUE: One assessment concept we pursued was in creating student-and teacher-selected portfolios. I asked the students to select examples from a 9-week period of what they thought represented their best work in various categories. Those categories ranged from a piece of work they were proud of to something they were still wondering about. They were asked to write a short expla-nation of why they chose particular pieces of work, and from these explanations I gained insight to the value students placed on certain aspects of the curriculum. Later, these portfolios were shared with students' parents.

A final piece of the assessment pie came as a result of dialogue sessions in which we teachers asked ourselves: "Are we really giving the children what they need?" "How do we know?" A discussion with Chris, Delia, and ECC Project staff member Anna Loebe about "dispositions," or what we believe about edu-cation and what we value for our students, resulted in a tool that I found useful. It is a list of my beliefs about what I want children to be able to do, as well as feelings (or dispositions) that I believe are important for them to develop, such as curiosity, love of learning, persistence. I wanted to paint a picture of each child as a learner. As I developed this list, it gave me a chance to look at each student individually, at least once a quarter, and think about how the program I was providing helped him or her achieve those goals. Although I'm not sure that it's anything more than a checklist, at least it's a beginning.

Also as a result of dialogue, Laura and I created a similar tool to help us look at our overall program. So I conclude at this point that assessment for me is a way of asking myself various ques-tions, such as: Am I providing what children need in order to succeed in later years? Are children growing in knowledge and are positive changes taking place? Do the children recognize and acknowledge their own growth? Are parents and the community able to see and value these changes?

Reflections

Teachers emphasize here the important characteristics of portfolios and other alternative assessment activities that reflect contextualized curricula and take into account the advantage of promoting the first language of students as well as a second language. Most norm-referenced tests use only English. At Ochoa, the implications of this characteristic of norm-referenced tests meant that children with limited fluency in English were disadvantaged and could not accurately be assessed for what they knew or had learned. Also, bilingual students who had more strengths in Spanish than in English did not have the opportunity to perform in their areas of strength. Marianne, Becky, and Delia have found that portfolios and other alternative assessment activities promote the use of both Spanish and English. Linda found it helpful to share the task of evaluation with the students themselves.

Ana points out that attention to assessment has provided ways for her own reflection about what she does and why. Her attention to alternative assessment has encouraged her to sit down each day at the end of school and ask how the day went and how her interactions with children proceeded. Ana and others have rejected an old purpose for assessment—that of sorting children by comparing them with other students. Instead, they are using criteria in judging what children know and do.

Ana, Chris, Delia, Laura, and Sue note that assessment has also included examination of the nature of the school and the classroom programs. In a manner similar to using criteria to evaluate children's work, the work of teachers has undergone scrutiny. Chris notes that various dispositions teachers promote can serve as criteria for the examination of learning opportunities—that is, development of children's curiosity, opportunities for students to reflect on their theories, connections between parents/the community and the school/children.

The new assessment processes—portfolios and other activities—share a set of characteristics that seem to run through much of what the teachers have learned from the assessment developments undertaken thus far:

1. Each provides vehicles for children to assess their own strengths and weaknesses.
2. Students assist in the establishment of the criteria for judging their productions and products.
3. Student involvement in the assessment activity consists of the common threads of analyzing, interpreting, and recording what they find out.
4. Students assess themselves and their peers, using the shared and agreed-upon criteria.
5. The criteria of assessment that students and teachers use in the evaluation of learning activities also guide the development of every activity. These criteria then turn into guides for what teachers and learning activities promote.
6. Teachers have undertaken involvement of parents and other community members with the children in examining the children's productions and products and their thoughts and ideas underlying these actions.

There is much more to be examined and learned about assessment at Ochoa (and other schools involved in the ECC Project). To that end, in 1994, the project established an Assessment Advisory Group, comprised of seven educators and researchers from throughout the country who have expertise in assessment practices. This panel meets semiannually with the teachers, principal, parents, schoolchildren, and/or area community/business leaders, each of whom is asked to suggest, examine, and explore a variety of practices and procedures that will provide greater integrity in assessing the knowledge and skills of children in ECC Project schools and elsewhere.

10

Involving Parents in School Reform

Parents of children at Ochoa are viewed by school faculty very differently now than they were when the project began. Daily they are discovered to be a resource for classroom work; their knowledge, perhaps because it is different from the knowledge of parents who are considered middle-class, is seen as a valuable asset to be used and encouraged. At the same time, the knowledge and skills that children acquire at home and bring to school are the foundation on which curriculum can be built and new knowledge and skills can be acquired. In general, parents are interested in their child's schooling and often know the particular needs, weaknesses, and strengths of children in their own neighborhood. Thus, their involvement in their children's education is encouraged by teachers, further carrying out the meaning of the ECC Project's concept of indigenous invention.

At the time the project began in 1990, parental involvement throughout the country seemed to be guided by a conventional question—how to rectify the apparent shortcomings of poor parents, such as most whose children attended Ochoa. In their efforts to improve education, their focus often appeared to be directed at what changes parents could make in how they (the parents) support education and the way that they enact their roles as parents. Some efforts sought changes in the relationship between the school and family/home through workshops at the school or in a home, to provide opportunities for parents to learn about the "right way" to raise and educate their children. The workshops provided information about what parents can do to help their children with homework and ways to parent, including educational activities that these parents could undertake in their homes.

More recently, schools have sought provision of integrated services of health care and other governmental human services at the school for parents and poor families. In each of these examples, the school furnishes something to parents whom the school presumes lack something. By providing these "somethings," it is presumed the parents', families', and communities' educational deficits will diminish.

The ECC Project attends to parents and their relationships to project schools, but with a different orientation toward what that relationship should be. To make connections between and among families and educational institutions in the community suggested to us a different strategy from parent-education programs in which parents and families are seen as being in need of parenting skills to prepare their children for school. Instead, we took the position that families and children, although economically poor, were the best that they could be when the children came to school. Schools had to be ready and prepared for these children and their families.

Poor families have much knowledge and many skills and know a lot about their community and the world. This knowledge may differ from middle-class knowledge, but it is significant and is the foundation of children's knowledge prior to schooling. If schools build on these funds of knowledge, economically poor children will be advantaged by their circumstances and prior knowledge as they acquire new knowledge and skills in school and other educational institutions.

As in many schools, the teachers at Ochoa viewed parents as important in supporting the education of the children. However, they had a view which suggested that these particular parents had shortcomings and therefore could not adequately support the education of their children in the manner of more well-to-do parents. For example, many of the parents did not speak English. Some did not have legal immigration status. Some did not appear to appreciate the educational efforts of the school. These parents did not often come to school nor did they appear to know the school curriculum materials enough to help their children with their schoolwork. The school and the teachers have changed many of the views that they had about the parents.

The project made three assumptions about parents and their relationship to the school:

1. Parents have much to offer the school and the education of their children. They do not have to be "straightened out" or corrected by teachers, the school, or other public or private agencies.

2. Luis Moll (1991), a colleague at the University of Arizona, has suggested that economically poor families have funds of knowledge that have equivalence to the funds found in middle-class families. The knowledge and resources of these economically poor families have complexity and power; hence, the families do not have deficits. They have many resources to benefit children and their education. The project embraced this view and sought to build and use these funds of knowledge and the resources of the family in the education of the children, rather than to change these resources.

3. Poverty *does* bring on conditions in a community that require attention: fewer high-status and high-wage jobs, poor housing with regard to the numbers and quality of housing available, and inadequate medical and human services in the immediate area of the neighborhood. Unfortunately, the political life of a poor community usually has little utility in promoting access to political and other material resources for families and their neighbors. In effect, residents of poor communities, including the children, may have little confidence in themselves to make substantial differences and changes in the economic, personal, and civic matters of their communities. Such a condition does not bode well either for the individuals or for the democratic civic life of the United States's urban centers.

Based on these assumptions, the project first engaged a staff member to work in community organization. As a result, a core group of parents and neighborhood residents formed a community coalition. As the fifth year of the project began and its efforts were expanding to additional schools, a broader range of community involvement seemed appropriate. At that time, the project joined with the Pima County Interfaith Council (PCIC), a Tucson-based community-organizing effort of the Industrial Areas Foundation/Southwest. This PCIC-ECC Project partnership seeks encouragement of political action by parents of children in the project schools, and other neighborhood residents, and a shift in school curriculum so that students and their parents study and investigate matters of importance to their well-being. In so doing, teachers, parents, and students seek understanding of these local community circumstances, doing their investigations and work in the persona of scientists, mathematicians, historians, and the like. As they seek and find solutions to local problems, they together advocate for changes in their community structures.

This focus on strategy and curriculum builds on what children and their families know best: their families and neighborhoods, which are their areas of expertise. As they make changes, they directly improve their family and neighborhood life. Undertaking such work also manifests itself in changes and improvements in community life, providing additional motivation and value to this kind of activity.

In the context of these ideas, then, the ECC Project and the teachers, parents, principal, and students of Ochoa have sought new relationships among all of these constituents, especially the relationships of parents to the school and schooling of their children.

DELIA: I have had to reexamine the meaning of parental involvement, especially in the context of Ochoa's primarily Hispanic student enrollment. Parental involvement used to mean something like parents and teachers meeting at an Open House, where only English was spoken. (My Spanish had become rusty through years of not using it.) Anyway, the parents were not to know too much, so they were not told much. Neither their culture nor their language was respected, and they weren't invited to play an active role in their child's schooling—unless, of course, it was a matter of raising money for something or other. Often parents were viewed as troublemakers who might start trying to make decisions that we teachers did not favor.

As I reexamined the work of the teacher and the work of the student in the restructuring of school, I realized there was a broader responsibility for a child's education. I should not accept sole responsibility for the education of children; parents and community had a responsibility, too.

During a weekly dialogue session, Chris and I presented our experiences in having parents volunteer to participate as teachers and resources. This was hard for some of the teachers to accept. There were comments about parents disrupting the classroom when they showed partiality to their child, and some teachers felt that parents would be there just to criticize what the teacher was doing. I felt there was a general attitude that Hispanic parents couldn't possibly have anything to contribute to a school setting. There was the comment, "Many of them don't even speak English." Chris and I persisted in our belief in parental involvement and were continually impressed by parents' insights when they shared their knowledge with the children.

For example, as a follow-up to the pumpkin study unit that Chris describes in Chapter 6, our classes visited the home of one of the children. The mother of the child showed the children how to make pumpkin *empanadas* [turnovers]. While that demonstration was under way, another mother who was present organized a science experiment, teaching the refraction of light. Her equipment was simply a paper-roll tube and aluminum foil. She also talked to the kids about health and nutrition, sanitation in cooking, and personal hygiene. Then all of the children participated by making one or two pumpkin turnovers for themselves. The parents also explained all kinds of cooking ingredients and discussed the cultural aspects of cooking, explaining the differences in foods in various parts of Mexico. All in all, it was a good learning experience for everyone, and Chris and I felt the parental involvement was a very good thing.

Another example involved the grandmother of two brothers in our classroom, who meets the boys at our doorstep every day after school. You can read "hope" in her eyes. When we decided to study mesquite trees and shrubs, which are native to Mexico and our area of the United States, we asked her to talk with the class about the varieties of mesquites, the physical characteristics, and the physical attributes of the plant in different stages. She did all of that as well as talk about the medicinal value, the cosmetic uses of mesquite, and the advantages of cooking with mesquite wood.

For Halloween, the class went to her house and played games, ate lunch, sang songs, and socialized. The mother of another student was there and told ghost stories and talked about the history of Halloween customs in Mexico.

I pondered how I could relate more to the community and especially to parents to help them redefine their roles and responsibilities in the education of their children. After all, through the years they had also been conditioned to act a certain way in relation to school. The hard part was how to begin being a social being with other social beings known as parents. Even the names of our gatherings for parents were cold: Open House, Parent-Teacher Meetings, Parent Conferences. So my teammate, Ana, and I settled on calling our gatherings *cafecitos* (coffee klatches). It sounded cozy, inviting, and social. Then I thought, why can't we just speak normally in either Spanish or English, whichever works better for communication? We asked parents to suggest the time and day that was best for them to meet, and the cafecitos became a reality.

Initially, warm coffee and warm pastries on a chilly winter morning were magnets for bringing parents to school, but soon respectful and friendly relationships began to develop and grow into powerful and productive learning experiences. Coffee and pastries became just a trimming. Today, there is a feeling of camaraderie among those of us who attend. Those who are unable to attend the cafecitos communicate with others via telephone or update others in the school hallways or as they walk home with their children after school. Sometimes they stop by the classroom for a few seconds just to say "Hi," and the core group periodically suggests ideas for a new project stemming from their interests and strengths; we work together as a team of parents and teachers with similar goals and a mutual interest in making school a better place for their children.

It boggles my mind how the institution of education cannot seem to see the importance of parent and community resources in making learning effective.

LINDA: Even though I believe that parental involvement is an integral part of school reform, I feel as though I accomplished little in this area. I did find that by combining the intermediate grades and teachers advancing with students from grade to grade provides more opportunities for teachers to get to know parents and therefore better understand their students.

I did make some effort to get parents involved in the "Lot Project" after our students appeared before the City Council [see Chapter 6] and Ochoa faculty and students acquired responsibility for development of the vacant lot. I invited parents and other community members to attend a "lot presentation" that students and teachers scheduled in conjunction with the Tucson Audubon Society and the ECC Project. At school, the students had been engaged in answering such questions as: "What is this lot like before we make any changes?" "What does this information tell us?" and "How can this information be helpful in our future planning?" The study plan was divided into four categories: soil, living things, history, and human uses.

A number of parents and other adults did show up for the lot presentation and helped students set up the public address system, easels, and tables for their displays and other evidence of their learning. Unfortunately, the weather wasn't cooperative that day. The wind was blowing hard; it was chilly, and finally it rained. So we all scrambled to get the displays back inside the school to avoid water damage. That was near the end of the school year, shortly before my transfer from Ochoa to a magnet middle school, so I really didn't have an opportunity to reschedule the activity during better weather.

During the third year of the project, after Becky and Sue had completed the project on insects (described in Chapter 6, this volume), they invited parents to view an exhibit and demonstration that the children had prepared. Following are some of the significant comments recorded in the parent dialogue session that took place during the parents' visit (names of the children have been changed):

Sue: Thanks for coming. [We want to share with you our] belief about getting kids excited in the classroom, learning with their hands, asking questions and reading books to answer their questions. The children examined insects and asked questions, and then we decided which questions about insects were most important in their lives.

Becky: Some of their questions came after they saw a video or used a microscope. We grouped their questions and kids found the answers. The presentations [today] don't show all the information the children have. They are more natural in class, and we see so much enthusiasm and knowledge.

Maria's Mother: The children are coming home and talking about what they know. "I learned this," [they say]. Maria likes insects. She saw a black widow and said, "Mom, don't touch it. It can hurt you."

Becky: And the children are so confident about what they know.

Maria's Mother: She was telling me that some insects you can touch and some you can't. Some are poisonous and some are not. They're really learning.

Becky: Irma is an expert. She will pick up bugs that no one else will.

Irma's Mother: I kept hearing about *manducas*. I wondered, "What's that?"

Sue: Irma's word is *cephalothorax*. The children took a [state-required] 6-day test that happened to be on insects. The text talked about the head, chest, and stomach—talking down [to the children]. They said, "That's wrong; that's a head, thorax, and abdomen." And Irma asked, "Where's the cephalothorax?"

Irma's Mother: She showed me a mealworm and said that's what gets in macaroni and cheese.

Becky: Here are some of the journals that the children kept every day.

Sue: We asked them to be scientists. They had to measure and weigh the manducas. They saw the manducas grow and change and move through the wandering stage. Then they began shrinking. They were wondering why the changes were happening. They were excited.

Sarah's Sister: Sarah comes home every night and talks and talks about what she did. She's always looking for bugs. She wanted my makeup bottles to hold them in. She picks bugs up and talks about them.

Sue: The kids feel really powerful. It used to be we taught science from a book. . . . Now they actually touch things, talk about what they observe. They really know things. It's really important, this new way of "knowing."

Becky: They measured how a grasshopper jumps. They recorded it in different ways and used a graph. They used tiles to find the average length of the jumps. They were doing lots of math and science and reading for information.

Sue: Here are the stories the children wrote about insects. We put them on computer so they could edit them.

Becky: We're going to make a class book so the children can take the stories home.

Chris also was participating in the parent dialogue session and chose this opportunity to ask some questions of the parents:

Chris: We're teaching a different way. Do you think it's better? How can we explain the difference we're seeing?

Irma's Mother: The children are not sitting. The children found out things by themselves. The teacher isn't talking but is only supervising. Irma doesn't usually get excited very much, but she talks about this every day. She comes home and finds bugs every day.

Maria's Mother: This way is better. They are finding the words. They read the words; they write the words.

Becky: They have a reason to read.

Maria' s Mother: They try their best because it's interesting to them.

Becky: If we just tell them, they don't remember.

Irma's Mother: The other way is boring. This way is exciting.

Maria's Mother: They're doing the best they can because they're excited. Maria is reading things now, and she likes it. She doesn't forget. When they're interested, they remember.

Sarah's Mother: Before, Sarah was finicky. She never would touch a bug. Now she loves it.

Becky: That's right. At the beginning of the year we took a survey. Only two kids said "Yuck" about bugs, and Sarah was one of them. Now she has more containers and jars of insects than anyone. What we're doing is called *inquiry*. It's a new way of teaching and there's a lot of new research about it. Kids learn more when they're excited and responsible for their own learning.

Pedro's Mother: Pedro comes home and looks for bugs everywhere. He's turning the house upside down looking for them. He goes around investigating. He wants to know why. He looks at the cat and thinks of how it's related to the rat. He wants to know how the dog is related to the rat.

Becky explained that he was investigating the food chain and how animals are interrelated.

Pedro's Mother: He was looking at the ladybugs on the rose bushes and said they eat the bugs that eat the plants. He said how wonderful it is that they have bugs that eat the problem animals.

Chris continued with her questions to parents.

Chris: We're struggling with the idea of how to report to parents what children know. Do report cards help? Does this way [exhibits of work] help? Report cards take a lot of time, and we wonder if there's a better way.

Maria's Mother: Report cards are just letters. They don't tell us how much the kids know. What does "excellent" mean? What do the children need?

Pedro's Mother: I'd rather watch the children investigate.

Sarah's Sister: Sarah gets good grades, but more important is what she says at home about what she does in the classroom. We see her at home studying, experimenting, climbing trees to study bugs. Report cards show some, but listening to her tells more.

Sarah's Mother: The report card has just numbers and symbols.

Pedro's Mother: Yes. They are just numbers and symbols. What you are teaching the children is very important—the consequences of bug bites.

Irma's Mother: The one thing I could tell from her last report card was that she was happy.

Becky: How else can we help tell you?

Irma's Mother: People need to come to school and ask and see.

Sarah's Mother: The conferences were good.

ANA: In the chapter on assessment, I mentioned that Delia and I write down the comments of the children during the school day and they are helpful in assessment. In addition, the children's comments are sent home to communicate to parents what is happening in our classrooms. We feel this is one way to keep parents updated as well as involving them in reflecting with their child. I feel it is important for parents to have input and to reflect with their children regarding their learning. This creates more communication between the parent(s) and the child. These reflections may even guide the direction of our classroom curriculum.

DELIA: Our team began to narrow the gap between home and school by sending out a monthly newsletter with information about classroom events and student activities. The newsletter announces meetings and lists needs for special materials. For instance, when we had a vehicle project, we asked for "beautiful" junk that the kids could build with. We also send out a "Home and School Connection" flyer with ideas on how the parents can help their children learn at home about the theme we are studying. It gives specific "how-to's" and points out some of the skills the child is learning while doing specific activities.

One of our team members suggested that we put a bulletin board outside our classroom where we could post information for parents. At one of our parent coffee hours we mentioned that we didn't have a means for fastening it to the wall, and one of the fathers volunteered to bring his drill and put up the board. Parents seem to like the bulletin board; we see them reading it while they wait for their kids to be dismissed from school at the end of the day.

SUE: At our parent-teacher conferences, Laura and I had the children share with their parents the portfolios they had created [see Chapter 9, this volume]. Together we looked at the students' justification for their choices in the portfolios and at how the students evaluated their own work for the 9-week period. Because I work mostly in units that integrate reading/language, writing, math, science, and so on, I listed the activities we had conducted during the quarter under these classifications. Seeing lists of all the work helped the parents know exactly what their child had been involved in during the quarter.

Communication with the parents at the classroom level is critical. At one Parent-Teacher Conference, I was aware that one of my students' parents was coming in with an "agenda." She was concerned that her child was not getting weekly spelling lists to study. Both research and my own experience has convinced me that weekly lists do not make better spellers, but opening a conference with such a statement, I believed, would have led to immediate conflict. Instead, I opened by letting her child share his portfolio of work and explain why he valued it. I was able to show how the student had changed and grown since the year before, and I let each student share his self-evaluation of his work for the past quarter. By the end of the conference, when I gave her the report card, I asked her if she had any questions, and she said I had answered all of her concerns. We never did talk about spelling.

Using the portfolios and each child's self-evaluation, I asked each of the children to give himself or herself a grade on the traditional report card. I also filled out their report cards, based on all the information we had gathered. At the end of the parent conference, I gave the parents the report cards. Most of them barely looked at the report cards; with all of the other information, they knew what their child was doing at school. I asked the parents which was most important, the students' self-evaluation and portfolios or the traditional report card. All but one indicated that they had a better picture of their child from the former, although several said they still wanted to see a "report card."

LAURA: I was one of the teachers who believed that parents in the classroom were more disruptive than an asset. I had no idea how to utilize their knowledge and expertise in the classroom. I thought they were just an added problem who would occasionally make dittos for me. I've probably learned more than my students with regard to not only understanding parents and their needs, but also appreciating their involvement. I would like to have more.

I never use parents as volunteers to do the mundane or menial work. I've realized that they're far more valuable. I've had parents teach and interact with the students and assist in the classroom activities. Parents have taught classes in a variety of subjects, from making tortillas to the multiple uses of cacti. They have told stories to the class and shared their family histories. It's fascinating listening to students explain to adults how they discovered an answer to a problem, and then having the adult respond with how he or she approached it. Everyone is welcome in our classroom, but no one is allowed to just sit and observe.

The powerful influences in a child's life obviously must include parents and grandparents. To be able to include them in the classroom increases the child's knowledge and understanding of himself or herself. One of the things I found to be extraordinary is the desire for the children to share items, pictures, and stories about their families and themselves. We have allowed time to explore ourselves and our families, especially during the last couple of years. Many times this engages the parents in the classroom activities, even if they're not able to be present. Occasionally, their absence is due to the parent being in prison. It is incredible to share their letters and cards. I've also had the opportunity to meet several of the imprisoned parents when they were released. They enjoyed becoming part of their child's life in school, and they continue to do so.

SUE: In a perfect world, parents, teachers, and the community would all agree on what was best for students in terms of curriculum, methodology, and assessment. In reality, each faction comes with its own set of experiences and beliefs that guide their thinking.

Parents are the children's first teachers in terms of language, cultural heritage, and values. Children bring with them vast amounts of information about their world, tempered through the eyes of their environment. As a teacher, I also come into the classroom bringing my own collection of experiences and beliefs and expectations. Is it any wonder that we sometimes find ourselves looking at this place called "school" in different ways?

In our work with the ECC Project, we are committed to finding ways to make school a better place for students. This necessarily involves change, and change is scary . . . scary for teachers who risk putting their long-held beliefs on the table to be examined by others in the light of current research. It's even scarier for parents, who see the changes, but without input from us teachers, don't know why the changes are being made. Conflicts can come with change.

The key to avoiding that type of conflict has to be communication among teachers, parents, students, and the wider community. The more parents and the community are involved in schooling, the better the chance for understanding and meaningful support for change.

At the classroom level, teachers need to involve parents and children in a continuing dialogue about the changes we are trying to make. One program that has created real understanding and support is Family Math or Family Science. Parents are invited to the school for a series of three or four programs in which they and their children participate in using the new math and science curricula. Then, in dialogue with the teachers and Title 1 support teachers, they share feelings and opinions and raise questions about what they have experienced.

Reflections

Teachers have told stories in this chapter about the changed views of parents and the new relationships that teachers and parents have cultivated in the Ochoa neighborhood during the past 5 years. In addition, teachers also have explained the contrasting experiences that they have had with parents and families as they have recently viewed parents as capable, full of knowledge, and interested in what their children experience in school, as compared to earlier views of parents as incapable, in need of parent education, and providing inadequate support for schoolwork at home. For example, the grandmother of two brothers in Delia's classroom became a resource about mesquite trees and shrubs. She shared her knowledge of these trees and their use as a medicine and a cosmetic. Delia came to see this grandmother and others like her as a resource, which in turn sparked the idea of the cafecitos.

Two threads then run through this chapter about these new experiences with parents. The first thread represents what has happened when teachers viewed parents in positive terms and used the strengths that each parent has and that children bring with them to school. For example, the language of Spanish-speaking parents has become an asset. The school now conducts all meetings with parents in Spanish and English. One language does not prevail in these school meetings with parents. Instead, the language that parents want to use determines the medium of expression of these meetings.

The second thread exemplifies what happens when productive relationships develop between parents and teachers, and how such relationships support the ongoing development of children. As parents have experienced the new work that children have undertaken, they became advocates for the changes that are under way in the school. These parents saw that their children had acquired new knowledge and skills and positive views of themselves, their learning, their teachers, and their school.

For example, Becky and Chris provide views regarding what these parents have observed and discussed with their children about the insect investigations. Irma's mother observed that her daughter, on her own, had discovered things about bugs and had been excited about learning about them. Pedro's mother observed similar activities on Pedro's part. Because of these experiences, most parents viewed report cards as no longer meaningful. Pedro's mother and others preferred watching the children investigate.

In a similar manner, when parents participated in family mathematics and science activities at the school, they came to understand the importance of new views of mathematics and science, and their support of these changes increased significantly.

These parental responses suggest several facts about relationships between parents and teachers at Ochoa. For example, teachers had confidence in parents to respond thoughtfully to questions about what, if anything, they had observed in their children during the insect investigations. They also showed an openness to what parents say about what their children are learning and their analyses of report cards and other ways of assessing children that may provide better information than report cards.

Such positive parental responses to educational changes at Ochoa contrast sharply with the conventional views of parents who will not accept significant alterations in school structures and activities. As these Ochoa parents participated in more equal relationships with teachers, and watched and participated with their children in new school activities, they viewed the classroom changes at Ochoa as powerful and educative. They valued these new activities for some of the same reasons that teachers valued them.

Reference

Moll, L. C. (1991). *Vygotsky and education: Instructional implications and applications of sociohistorical psychology.* New York: Cambridge University Press.

11

Risk Taking in the Role of the Principal

The project had the good fortune to have a strong, intelligent, and competent administrator in its first participating school (and for that matter, in subsequent participating schools). Throughout this book, teachers have expressed their appreciation for their leader in risk taking, Elsa Padilla. In this chapter, Elsa reveals her own beliefs and ideas about what it takes to pioneer a project with goals to rethink everything that goes on at the school and, in most cases, change conditions so that teaching practices, school structures, and curricula can be reinvented. In her thinking and actions, she took risks that allowed for the possibility of failure.

Without Elsa Padilla as principal of Ochoa Elementary School, the ECC Project would not have developed in the fashion that it has during these past 5 years. Her contributions to project accomplishments demonstrate the significance of a principal in promoting or interfering with positive and worthwhile change and student learning in schools. In Elsa's case, she promoted worthwhile change among teachers, in the relationships between parents and teachers, and in her thoughts and actions as a principal.

At the same time, neither she nor I will argue that she caused the changes or student learning; rather, her thoughts and actions as the principal constituted an aspect of the configuration of contributing factors that promoted new thoughts and actions among teachers, children, and parents in the school and neighborhood. Nevertheless, without her contribution to this configuration of factors, the configuration and the other factors would have had less power to promote educational reinvention.

In the beginning, when determining which school would begin the work of the project, I sought a school where the principal could promote the purposes and ideas of the project and serve as a partner with me in promoting project goals as one of the preconditions. Within minutes during the first conversation with Elsa about her interest and willingness to participate, I was elated. Here was a person who had only served as principal for less than a year but who had the intelligence and wisdom of a veteran administrator. In addition, she also had what seemed to be the most essential qualities: (a) an expressed commitment to challenge what education had been and to urge what it could be, (b) a deep respect for and belief in the children to achieve in school and benefit from their education beyond schooling, and (c) that same respect for and belief in the families of the neighborhood in supporting that education.

Elsa also expressed willingness to challenge what she and her colleagues in the school and district would see as normal schooling and district business. In effect, Elsa talked and acted like a risk taker. She would take risks to enact her values and commitments to the children, parents, and teachers of Ochoa School, and yet not to be different just for the sake of being different and innovative.

In these next pages, Elsa discusses these commitments and beliefs that she held, as we began our work together, and what she now has learned about undertaking this kind of work as a principal who took risks within the project during the past 5 years.

My Role as Principal in an ECC Project School
by Elsa N. Padilla

Becoming a principal at Ochoa Elementary School provided the opportunity for me to work at a school in which most of the students were at risk and few believed that they would be successful in their adult life. I felt confident that they could be successful learners in spite of such obstacles as low family income and limited—or lack of—the English language. I knew that continuing with traditional educational practices that had failed in the past was not the way to get Ochoa students to be lifelong learners, empowered and able to set high goals and achieve them.

The job was complex, and observation became my obsession as I attempted to identify problems and issues and change the educational environment. The teachers were excellent and seemed open to different ideas because they really cared about the children. Students and parents appeared to be motivated for learning, but why wasn't it happening? The more I thought about it, the more I began to realize that the role of the principal had to change if changes were to occur throughout the school. Once I realized that everything—yes, everything—needed to be examined, including myself, I started questioning why I did things a certain way. Would the style of my leadership promote or inhibit change?

Looking back, I see my first year as a time in which I got to know the parents, students, and staff, identifying areas of concern, providing support to teachers, and examining how my role might fit my two primary goals, which were

1. Empowerment of teaching staff, parents, and students
2. Encouragement of each person to be successful and a lifelong learner

With these goals in mind, one question before me was: "Could I do it?" Knowing full well that change could not be mandated, and that our students, teaching staff, and parents deserved better, my second question was: "How will I do it?"

During the last semester of my first year, a district administrator asked if I would work with Dr. Paul Heckman and his staff in a foundation-funded program to reinvent elementary school education. That program, of course, was the Educational and Community

Change Project. Paul Heckman and I discussed the philosophy and goals of the project, and I could not believe how lucky I was to find someone who had the same vision I had and who proposed some very interesting notions about the process of change.

After presenting the idea of the project to the staff, we all agreed that change was needed, but we needed support throughout the process. I still remember that staff meeting when teachers verbalized why change needed to occur. I could not believe it; the views of the staff were the same as mine. Then it dawned on me: I was right in that I couldn't do it alone, but having everyone involved in creating changes was the way we could accomplish our common goals. I felt that the thousand-pound load on my back was reduced to a weight I could manage.

It was great to know that all of us were identifying areas of concern; we were all willing to reach common ground by working together; but I felt that was not enough. I did some reflecting on my own life and career. When I was a teacher, my principal supported me, encouraged me to take risks, and allowed me to make mistakes and learn from them. I came to see the role a principal must play if true change was to take place. Even though I had read many books and articles on leadership, it was not until I was able to pull back and reflect on my own beliefs, practices, and experiences that the picture became clearer. I realized that I had become empowered as a teacher, a diagnostician, a central staff administrator, and now as a principal by having the good fortune to work with supervisors who allowed me to be a responsible risk taker. They encouraged and supported me and, best of all, they gave me permission to fail. With permission comes mutual trust—a must for true change to occur.

A question I am often asked is whether we selected teachers for this project and got rid of teachers who did not see a need for changes to be made. The answer is "no." The philosophy of the project is that you take a school "as is." What is critical is to create an environment in which change can occur and not to force people to change (which I believe cannot be done anyway).

In the beginning, when the entire Ochoa faculty agreed that the ECC Project should come into our school, most of the teachers were very enthusiastic and curious; however, there were those with less enthusiasm. As the project continued through the next 5 years, there were periodic dropouts of faculty members—teachers saying that reinvention required too much work, they were out of the classroom too much, they were experiencing burnout, or they needed time to regroup their thinking about what they had been doing and would be doing in the future. This raises the question of what role the administrator plays with the nonparticipating teachers.

After the first months of the project, I arrived at four premises that I believe hold true for participating and nonparticipating teachers:

1. All teachers want the best for their students.
2. Communication among all staff members is very important, and I, as the administrator, am responsible for creating opportunities for all of the staff to communicate with each other.
3. Each teacher deserves support from the administrator.
4. Each of us has the capacity to change and improve, but my role is not to change people. It is to create a school environment that promotes examination of ideas, risk taking, exploration of new strategies and topics. In this environment, change becomes the norm, and more and more teachers will decide on their own the types of changes they want to make.

With change, other aspects of administration are impacted; the evaluation of teachers is one. A typical evaluation involves the teachers selecting a lesson for the administrator to observe, a discussion of the observation followed by a written report. In such evaluations, many teachers fear that the administrator is looking for evidence that the teacher "needs fixing." It is logical, then, for a teacher to select a lesson he or she knows well—in other words, a lesson they can do in their sleep.

As I have changed how teachers are evaluated, I have moved to a process that mirrors the critical areas in the process of change. I ask the teachers to select an area in which they feel they want improvement, such as a more child-centered classroom, hands-on science, promoting empowerment of the students, and so on. In turn, this becomes the lesson I will observe during the teacher-evaluation process. This type of evaluation has significantly improved the quality of the dialogue between each teacher and me. All teachers are using this system for the evaluations, and last year some teachers asked to be evaluated as a team. This change in the evaluation process tells me that I am trusted by the staff, that I have been consistent with my permission to risk, and that the staff is willing to dialogue with me regarding areas they have identified as needing change.

As teachers are feeling empowered, they also are changing classroom practices that lead to empowerment of the students. A child-centered curriculum is emerging, and every school and classroom practice is being questioned by all to ensure that the students have permission to take risks: They have lots of support, permission to fail and then learn from their failure. This has been effective in the empowerment of the staff and myself.

The issue of empowerment of people who have been oppressed for a long time has extended to a third group, the parents. We—the teachers and I—believe that when parents are empowered, their quality of life improves and in turn their children are empowered and their lives improve.

Reflecting now on the past 5 years, some conditions for change have become key to our continuing change. It is difficult to summarize some of the changed conditions, but I would say that our goals and accomplishments include the establishment of an educational environment that

- is supportive of the faculty, students, and parents;
- encourages responsible risk taking;
- establishes trust among the school staff and the project staff;
- affords many, many opportunities for the staff and project personnel to question, as well as reflect on, educational practices on a weekly basis;
- recognizes that the empowerment of staff, parents, and students is a goal that is just as important as increasing academic achievement.

Our job is not finished, and perhaps it will never be. I realize more and more that the process of change is very slow. It takes time to change beliefs, theories, and practices and implement them in regular classroom work. However, hearing teachers say, "I will never teach the old way again," has made these years well worth the energy, work, and time spent, and I look forward to the years ahead, when we have the opportunity to continue the change process and discover an equitable way to assess the value of our efforts on behalf of the children, their parents, and their community.

Reflections

Elsa Padilla has related several key characteristics of her self as the project began. First, she had the intention and will to promote examination and reinvention of everything that constituted the school and her role as principal. She wanted to promote change in herself and in what others did in the school. Elsa discussed two goals that guided her during the early years of the project: (a) to promote the power of parents, students, and staff and (b) to encourage the success and lifelong learning of all of these individuals who made connections to the school.

Elsa also highlights a learning she acquired early in our work together—she and the teachers had similar ideas and wishes and wants for the school. However, she did not know of these mutual aspirations until we brought everyone together to discuss and explore these shared ideas and wishes. Neither the teachers nor Elsa knew that the other had similar aspirations and hopes for the school and student learning.

Elsa also has identified the interplay between trust and permission giving, which, in turn, has promoted further risk taking on the part of teachers at the school. In particular, she has discussed an often overlooked aspect of risk taking and permission to take risks—the permission to fail in our efforts to alter existing practices and structures. She encouraged teachers to try out new ideas and practices and, if in their eyes the attempt "failed," learn from what happened. Elsa encouraged teachers to learn from their actions, rather than to find the right answer for how to change schooling practices.

Finally, Elsa has shown the importance of the long-term view for schooling's ongoing reinvention. School reinvention does not happen once, rather it continues nonstop. Elsa ends her discussion with a tentative list of conditions that for her may promote such long-term continuous reinvention: (a) support of the teachers, students, and parents; (b) establishment of trust among the school and project staffs; (c) the importance of questioning and reflecting on all aspects of actions on a weekly basis; and

(d) the complementary interaction between empowerment of staff, parents, and students, as well as student achievement.

Even though the road to these accomplishments and insights has had bumps in it, Elsa shows the determination and commitment to continue the journey and experience the joy of school reinvention in the accomplishments of students, parents, and teachers.

12

Reflecting on Change
and Looking to the Future

In this final chapter, the authors offer brief essays explaining where each of them stands after 5 years in the project and how each views the prospects for the future. These essays will convey two important aspects of the many learnings of the project thus far: (a) Teachers, principals, parents, and children want powerful schooling and educational practices to prevail in schools, despite the fact that a narrow range of practices and structures has prevailed during the past century; and (b) the work of reinvention does not stop once teachers have altered aspects of education at a point in time; reinvention work continues into the future because new circumstances, opportunities, and insights will unfold as teachers, principals, parents, and students daily inquire into circumstances.

The Journey Begins
by Christine B. Confer

As I look back 6 years, I see a school that has changed profoundly. People work together much more closely than they did before they began participating in the ECC Project. We are no longer people who just happen to work in the same building; we're colleagues. We do not see ourselves as having "the answer," but rather we have many, many questions about how to achieve our goals.

And the goals that most of us aim for have shifted greatly: We want children to wonder about their world; to ask questions important for their lives; to find ways to answer their own questions; to identify, evaluate, and use resources; to rethink their theories in light of new perspectives and information; to communicate their findings in different media and different languages; and to evaluate their own learning. We also want to encourage dispositions that support learning, such as persistence, curiosity, and healthy skepticism. Last, but no less important, we want to support children as they grow in kindness, self-knowledge, self-acceptance, and the abilities to cooperate and live in a diverse, changing world.

But this is a huge, huge goal. It's scary to look at it in print. It's often scary to try to put into practice. There are so many things that hinder us, and it would be hard to succeed even if those hindrances did not exist.

However, it's even more scary to think about these children facing a life with few choices. When my own children were 5 years old, I would watch the 5-year-olds at Ochoa. Most of the children were no different from my own; confident, curious, loving, funny, sometimes silly. But if past statistics were to continue, half of the Latino children sitting near me would drop out of high school. Nine out of 10 of the Native American children would do likewise. Furthermore, most of these children's future socioeconomic levels could be far below those predicted for my own children.

There is no doubt in my mind that this situation is wrong. And I try to make sure that I am not part of the problem, that I help to create solutions and alternatives. But I also struggle continually. I struggle with issues of balance. This kind of work takes an incredible amount of time and energy. I have to keep my job in some kind of perspective. I need time with my own family.

The ECC Project has made great strides at Ochoa. I admire tremendously the people in the project with whom I have the great fortune to work. And yet, as with anything else in life, I see things that could be improved.

I often think that we teachers would benefit from more chances to be learners. I know that, for myself, I feel more confident when I have had opportunities to actually do things that scientists or historians or mathematicians do. I have a better sense of what kinds of activities those people take part in. I have a better sense of the perspective that a particular area provides. I am better able to articulate the learning that might result as well as the value of the process, because I have done those activities myself. Ochoa's teachers have had occasional chances to attend workshops through various Title 1 projects. I think that we need to continue to have these opportunities. I don't think that dialogue alone is sufficient, and I think we are still learning what other experiences are most helpful.

Also, as serious as our goals are, we have to not be overly serious. We have to allow ourselves to make the many mistakes that are part of the learning process. And we need to be able to be playful, because playful learners often come to the most innovative of conclusions. We need to have fun. We need to laugh.

I feel very fortunate to be a part of the ECC Project. I am learning a tremendous amount. The children at Ochoa are very fortunate to have caring teachers and rich experiences. And yet, there is a long way to go. The more we learn, the more questions we have. Even after 5 years and a lot of progress, it feels as if we have only just begun.

Thoughts on a Winter Eve
by Laura C. Fahr

I had always believed that school was a place *for* children. However, the reality of it seems to have been that it was a place to do things *to* children. When I transferred to Ochoa I discovered many alternative reasons for a school to be for children. There were—and are—students whose only meals are available at school, others who find refuge at school from abuse at home, warmth when it's cold outside, coolness when it's hot. It's a place where they receive some medical attention or sometimes clothes. We always have had reasons beyond the basics for providing school in the inner cities. Now, with rampant violence, gangs, and drugs, our school has to be the beacon lighting a road of safety and sanity for the children and parents of our community.

I know there are many teachers yearning or striving to change and improve education for their students. I know there are schools without university or administrative support attempting to change the culture of learning in their schools. I hope this book will provide the nurturing reinforcement to encourage and support those efforts.

In order for the ECC Project or the current conditions of education to exist at Ochoa, an extraordinary individual was required in the capacity of principal. There was no way I would try new, innovative, or different approaches without the absolute assurance of my supervisor that it was acceptable to risk these efforts. Elsa Padilla's strength, support, and trust have created the climate in which I can work. I always strive to do my best. It was easier under the old methods, but it's more fun and challenging now. I can never go back. This project could not survive without the support and risk taking of the administrators.

I think the future is always intrinsically involved with the past. Individuals we now regard as philosophers and geniuses were the ones who deviated from the norm. Schooling was established by the doctrine of the Church. It was dogmatic and autocratic, and, of course, only the privileged were educated. Individuals who disagreed or opposed the doctrine were at the least imprisoned and many were killed.

As schooling evolved, the same discipline was required to teach it as was used in the churches. Individuals who didn't function well or didn't have access were ostracized.

When publishing companies took over the process of education, they utilized the same format: memorize and regurgitate. This private industry took over mass production of education in much the same way as Ford did with cars. In order to convince people that it was the right way to "do" education, they invented standardized, norm-referenced tests to support the concept.

Of course, we also mandated compulsory education in the United States. I am convinced that the continuing imposition of textbooks, workbooks, standardized tests, and "basic skills" will inevitably result in the collapse of the educational system. I think this legalized idea of making all students fit into the same round hole is not only invalidating and eliminating students arbitrarily and capriciously, but with discrimination. The cultural biases, the language barriers and prejudices built into any standardized learning norm are ultimately destructive.

So, here we are in the ECC Project, trying to reinvent education. I suspect there are people who are as opposed to this as there were people opposed to Aristotle and Galileo—and others who are afraid of change and would deny access to Lincoln and Edison. But I'm not creating education for someone else to take into his or her classroom. I'm advocating that all teachers be given the opportunity and support to implement changes. What works for me at Ochoa will not necessarily work the same way down the street.

I'm not sure that everything I'm doing is right, but it is the best I can do at this time. I know my students are engaged and involved. I know that I am not alone. Not only do I have the support of my teammates, colleagues in our school district, and school administrators, but additionally I'm on-line with a network of 10 schools across the country who also are implementing changes.

What we're doing is not easy; there's no panacea. No one is going to be able to hand teachers answers to the problems in education, but we can't go back to textbook teaching. Things must change, and I support the right of teachers to create those changes.

A Beautiful Rainbow
by Ana Maria Andrade

My role has changed dramatically from the 5 years I was a Spanish reading resource teacher at Ochoa, working with students on a pull-out basis for individualized or small-group instruction. I still remember how lonely and isolated I felt my first year. Then after the ECC Project began, I teamed with an English reading resource teacher and worked in class with bilingual and nonbilingual teachers. Now, through my own choice, I am back as a regular classroom teacher enjoying a wonderful bilingual teaming experience with a colleague who has great visions for the future of our students.

The project's weekly dialogue sessions provide the opportunity for me to question, reflect, explore, and try out new practices. Reinvention, collaboration, and student-centered learning are promoted.

I have learned that empowering the students and providing opportunities for them to make decisions regarding their own learning have created a deep sense of responsibility and self-worth among our students. It's when their opinions are valued that meaningful learning begins to take place.

I feel confident that our 6-year-olds have a sense of self-worth. They feel ownership toward their learning; they're becoming independent learners and problem solvers and are inquisitive and enthusiastic about learning. Also, they are becoming respectful of diverse cultures and are acquiring both languages, Spanish and English.

My teammate and I find new ways of what Paul Heckman calls "working smarter" to help make our jobs sane and avoid burnout. This is very easy to do, because once we get involved in trying an idea we get very excited, and this enthusiasm acts like a natural rush and drives us to work diligently. This drive often leads us to working countless hours, so we continue to remind each other just how far our energy level can take us without getting too exhausted.

I have had wonderful teaching experiences in the past 18 years as a bilingual teacher and have established wonderful long-lasting friendships, but something new and exciting is happening within me now. It involves a special relationship between the students and myself. I find myself retreating from center stage in the classroom and discovering a new world among the 6-year-olds. I am relinquishing control, and it's okay. I have never enjoyed teaching more than now. My little friends can read, write, and problem solve, but not necessarily in our conventional way of understanding. We adults truly underestimate what children know, what they can do, or what they can understand. We have to learn to listen more with our hearts and look more closely with care and understanding—and then shoot for the stars.

I like the changes that have occurred within me. This fifth year, in particular, I find myself writing more about the exciting and meaningful "celebrations" in our classroom. I remember, when Paul Heckman first encouraged us to write about our experiences in reinventing education, that I thought I had nothing to contribute that would be of interest to others. I felt I was too busy and, frankly, writing was too much of a risk to take, because I did not see myself as a writer. During the past 5 years, a change has occurred. The positive encouragement that is always available from the ECC Project staff has led me to take the risk and write my stories regarding alternative education. In fact, I look forward to the end of each school day when I can sit down and write about how the day went. By doing this, I have become more reflective of what I do in the classroom and why.

I envision the Ochoa Elementary School students as a rainbow of beautiful colors reaching for the pot of gold that represents their learning potential. Then this very special rainbow will create a bridge of understanding, a bridge of light, and a bridge of hope for a better future. Contrary to the rainbow in the sky that soon disappears, my vision of the Ochoa rainbow of beautiful colors will be never-ending.

Looking for the Perfect Balance
by Rebecca Romero

Change is difficult at whatever point you may be in your life. At times, change can cause us to feel uncomfortable, it can cause us to doubt ourselves or deny that we need to change anything. When the project began I thought I didn't need to change anything I was doing in the classroom, but after these last few years, I feel I have changed in several ways. I have changed some teaching strategies and some attitudes, and I'm now questioning myself more as to why I'm doing what I'm doing.

One major concern I have, though, is that because we have this frame of mind to change, that teachers are changing everything, and some of these changes might exclude some very important learning that children need. I do believe that children need to have choices, that children need to have a voice in their learning, but children don't always know what they need to learn.

The teacher's role in the classroom must change, but the teacher cannot lose the role of guiding and facilitating children's learning. There needs to be a balance of children initiating their learning and teachers teaching. Not all children will choose to read or to write. Not all children can teach themselves to read, or they may not realize the importance of reading or writing until a later time. Reading and writing open up a child's world; we can make his or her world real through reading.

We have a great opportunity here at Ochoa to change, to experiment, and to take some risks, but we cannot forget that these children need to learn some very basic, important knowledge in order to be part of our society. Reading is one of the things I feel should not be left out. We as teachers need to create a learning environment that will stimulate learning, that will enable children to see learning as relevant to their world and cause children not only to be curious and to question their world, but to seek the answers to their questions.

The Search Goes On and On
by Suzanne Bishop

In college, one of my education professors asked us to write an autobiography. I remember being excited by the Japanese poetry form of Haiku at the time and selecting one short poem by Basho as the basis of my paper:

Experimenting . . .
I hung the moon on various
Branches of the pine.

I think my teaching career has been a series of experiments. We put on and take off many hats during our time with children. Each time the experiences have shaped and reshaped my thinking, leaving me a little different—sometimes happier, sometimes not, but never the same. With each change (third-grade teacher, Title 1 reading specialist, Higher Order Thinking Skills teacher, Essential Elements of Instruction trainer, and now a classroom teacher), there has been one goal: finding a way to make the world a better place for children. If I ever stop wanting to change and opt for "good enough," I hope I will have the courage to quit teaching.

During the past 5 years, my involvement with the ECC Project has added another chapter to my teaching career. We teachers at Ochoa accepted a challenge to reinvent school. Our weekly dialogue sessions have been a major influence on my journey—never easy, sometimes boring, often uncomfortable and full of conflict. Sometimes I feel as if dialogue has been an "I win, you lose" situation, or conversely, "You win, I quit." At times I have walked out hurting so badly that I would swear never to say another word: peace at any cost. But then there are those rare dialogue days when I come out knowing I am stronger for having risked sharing my deeply held beliefs, having had them tested and reshaped or made stronger.

I am not a person who makes decisions or changes quickly or easily. Change for me is a slow process; ideas have to muddle around in my head for a long time. But neither do I like conflict. An idea that is difficult for me is that it is better to debate an issue without settling it than to settle an issue without debating it. I have heard "good conflict" described as "heat and light without explosion." Maybe that is dialogue at its best. I know we won't always agree—but if we submit our hearts and minds to question what's best for children and teachers, maybe we can make a beginning.

In many ways our work is frustrating. We have worked hard for 5 years and have had the financial and emotional support of many people. So far, we've made changes, but not nearly enough. It's so easy to point fingers and say, "if only *they* [universities, parents, administrators] would do differently, things would be better." But I can't change others, only myself. If meaningful change is to occur, it has to start somewhere. I remember the words to the song: "Let there be peace on Earth, and let it begin with me." I've a few years to the end of my teaching career, but for the time that's left, I'll continue to try to make that difference.

The Many Definitions of Change
by Marianne Chavez

Now in my fifth year at Ochoa and fifth in the ECC Project, it's hard to believe that we're still not only trying to create conditions for change but also going through various implementation processes. We keep examining and questioning our ideas and practices, replacing some of them, and trying out new concepts. We're trying new class configurations and recreating the knowledge and skills we hope to promote. I often ask myself "How much longer will it take? Will we know when we get there?"

These questions mean I must work out my own meaning of the word *change*. There's always a certain amount of ambiguity and ambivalence, but I must repeatedly examine what I have been doing in order to know what it is I want to change. In other words, I ask myself "What am I doing in the classroom and why?" One thing is certain: Change means I have to let go of some of the old, familiar classroom circumstances, materials and practices—that is, text-books, worksheets, expectations for quiet in the classrooms, my control of the students at all times, and my having all the answers. It means sharing with other teachers instead of the isolation that was prevalent before. It means feelings of insecurity when I attempt to explain to visitors that what may appear to be chaos is actually a classroom of children (at least a majority of them) fully engaged in the project or topic under study.

Change means spending more time and energy planning class projects; it means listening to the children and allowing them to make decisions on what they need and want to learn. It means allowing and encouraging children to be critical thinkers, problem solvers, and risk takers. Change is about empowering everyone involved: students, parents, and myself.

Our dialogue sessions are important in promoting change and professional growth, although sometimes we are left with a feeling of hostility when we disagree in our beliefs, teaching practices, or general philosophies about teaching. But it's hard to believe that 5 years ago we teachers were working in isolation, not knowing each other—not knowing what was happening in any classroom other than our own. Through dialogue we got acquainted and developed a sense of trust as we started sharing what was going on in our classrooms. Dialogue also provides celebration when we share the neat things that are going on with children in the classrooms—or with their parents.

Dialogue seems to be creating a school that challenges everything that we're doing and recreating every aspect of education, and we teachers are creating what we believe to be valuable knowledge and skills—whatever they may be.

I have had wonderful experiences, including a project-related trip with Elsa Padilla and Paul Heckman to Köln, Germany, where we visited several schools that have multiage classrooms. Also, I value the experience of serving as acting principal at Ochoa for one semester. I can remember when Elsa told me she was planning to take a month of medical leave, tears were in her eyes as she pleaded with me to take her place during that time. I didn't know if I could handle the job, because, after all, I had no on-the-job experience in being a principal. My biggest fear was my possible failure to provide the moral support and inspiration Elsa had given all of us teachers in the project. She reassured me, and I said yes. Her anticipated

1 month extended to a full semester, from January through May. Fortunately, things held together well, and Elsa came back as principal in the fall.

Now as I think about where I started 5 years ago and what I'm doing now, I continue to wonder where I'm going and what the future of elementary education will be.

A Move to a New Dimension
by Delia C. Hakim

Five years ago, when the ECC Project started, I had dreams of change that would impact the universe—or so I thought. Five years later, I still have dreams, but on a smaller scale.

Initially I feared the unknown elements of change; the doubts were unbearable. I have since experienced the depths of change; change and I possess traits that are positive and negative, predictable and unpredictable, tolerable and intolerable. Change is interwoven with certainty and uncertainty—finding answers some of the time and accepting mystery at other times. Now, as I walk hand in hand with change, I feel a certain security. Change and I are not at odds with each other now. We are just following the natural flow of things.

Systemic change must occur, but it cannot happen overnight. In fact I don't believe it will happen during my lifetime. Visionaries can't do it alone, and change can't happen in isolation—one teacher, one school, one research project. Current projects for change may be likened to seismic jolts that make people run away and scream in fear. If we are to have systemic change, it must be like a rhythmic movement flowing across the country.

My incentive to change is based on what I believe to be my moral obligation to provide a more meaningful and productive education for all children, especially the children in my classroom. Traditional education is mediocre at best; it does not prepare children with the tools they need to survive and succeed in the world of today and the future. Traditional teaching is static, but the world is changing. I feel I am making my contribution to the change process. I continue my mission of digging for information/knowledge, so that I can enhance my passion for making learning—and life—better for students and myself.

Five years ago, the ECC Project was a green signal that lit only the tunnel's entrance; it was not the light at the end of the tunnel. There is no special formula for change; teachers cannot be forced or persuaded to change. Change is ongoing, and teachers must make a conscious decision to change.

Dialogue groups can reach an impasse. After 5 years of dialogue sessions, I feel they should evolve to meet the demands of each individual's personal needs and growth. I respect the fact that teachers are at different stages of growth, but I feel it is unproductive for me to be in dialogue sessions that examine the same things that were covered 5 years ago. My personal growth should be respected and I should be given the opportunity to develop in other important directions. Every inch of the journey has been exhausting and overwhelming—mentally, emotionally, and physically. Visionaries are a select few; risk takers are even fewer.

Tentatively, I plan to continue my trek. My hopes and efforts will be concentrated on my students. I will give serious thought to prioritizing my energies and not trying to be everything to everybody. I now carry emotional bruises and scars inflicted by others' jealousies, competition, criticisms, insecurity, and other negative human emotions. Unfortunately, these too are a natural part of life, but that kind of baggage helps me keep life in perspective.

I realize that I have stretched professionally and can never again really feel comfortable with my old teaching practices. I know that I have moved to a new dimension and can never go back to exactly the same time and place where I was 5 years ago.

I hope to continue on this grand journey with the expectation of giving up some and the anticipation of gaining much more. Though the path is long and unpredictable, I will watch for the next fork in the road and continue in a positive vein with whatever the future holds.

A Change of Place But Not of Heart
by Linda S. Ketcham

When Paul Heckman talked to us about the ECC Project 5 years ago, I had no idea that I would be transferred to another school 4 years later. Yet, here I am teaching sixth grade at a middle school which has an enrollment almost triple that of Ochoa. In addition to size, two things in the student enrollment stand out as different from Ochoa. One is that many or most of the students are from more affluent neighborhoods, and the second is the more balanced ethnicity of Anglos, Asians, Jews, and Latinos. Although the school allows some freedom from hard-core "traditional" practices, many of the things I'm required to do are the same as in my years before participating in the project. For example, old assessment practices and beliefs are prevalent, children are separated by language dominance, and students are pulled out of their regular classrooms for ESL and Special Education purposes. These examples are my driving force to continue my work in school reform.

One similarity to Ochoa is there are teaching teams. I have excellent teammates: One is a former colleague of Caroline Tomkins, the wife of Paul Heckman and a principal at an elementary school in Tucson. The other is Susanna Durón, the teammate at Ochoa I worked so closely with the first 2 years of the project, who returned to Tucson after 2 years in Alaska. I gave her name to the principal when he asked if I knew of a bilingual teacher who could work on my team; the rest is history. That's the good news.

The bad news is I miss the dialogue time that I had with teachers at Ochoa; I'm not getting the intellectual exercise that dialogue provided. Even as I began to write this short essay about my feelings, I felt a need for exchanging ideas with other teachers in the project. One of the things I learned through the project is that individuals have their own process of learning. When I began to put my thoughts together for this last chapter, I made a discovery about my own learning process. I realized that I am better at first verbalizing my thoughts and then putting them in writing. (I wonder how many of my students at Ochoa could have been better writers if they had first expressed themselves verbally.) With dialogue no longer a part of my work, I've made deliberate efforts to stay in touch with the ECC Project staff, and my participation in this book has helped in that area.

Also, I try to draw a few teachers in my new school together so we can bounce ideas off of each other, but the exchange and sharing time is sketchy, at best. Some of the teachers have heard about the project and ask very specific questions about it. I try to share what I can with them, but without the discipline of dialogue sessions, it's difficult to explore the basic beliefs and ideas we have. In that regard, I sometimes feel like a missionary without a church to back me.

The principal at my new school has been very supportive of my efforts, and there have been several opportunities for us to talk about such things as curriculum and assessment. I'm trying, and I believe succeeding, in staying within the bounds of what the administrator at my new school and the district require and expect. At the same time, I'm continuing to use some of the concepts that I acquired during my 4 years in the project. For example, I negotiate real work in my classes and try to get my students to work at problem solving, and I actively promote their self-regulation and self-responsibility. I practice and promote inquiry, encouraging students to have questions and to feel free to ask them and for the class to discuss them. Also I question everything that I do, because I feel it's the only way I can be sure that I'm doing by best. I'm trying to get a grasp on some innovative ways to encourage parental involvement, but I still find that difficult. I'm definitely trying to talk about some of the underlying beliefs that my teammates and I, as well as other teachers, have about what we're doing.

I would not have chosen to leave Ochoa, but I must admit that in the beginning I was relieved to think I would not have to deal with the ambiguity and anxiety that come with change. At the same time, I was saddened to leave the project. I was really passionate about the work we were doing, and I had learned—and was learning—so much. However, perhaps my transfer to another school makes it easier for me to realize how the project changed my beliefs and enhanced my understanding about teaching and how children learn. I will never go back to the beliefs I had when the project started.

Searching for the Answer to "Can It Be Done?"
by Paul E. Heckman

Throughout this book, my colleagues have illustrated, and I have discussed, their courage, successes, and frustration in seeking answers to the question that has guided our work together since 1990: Can it be done? Today, 5 years after the project's inception, the question remains in the forefront. I now have partial responses to the question, and the preceding chapters provide some of the support for my responses.

My emphasis on "partial" responses has importance, because a full response to this question will require further examination of efforts undertaken at Ochoa during the next few years, as well as at a second school, which has engaged in the ECC Project work during the past 3 years, and as of the fall of 1995, five Tucson schools will be fully engaged in the project.

Although the ideas of the project noted throughout this book have and will remain the guiding lights for this future work in project schools, I anticipate variation in what develops at each site, including the development of shared meanings, the issues that arise, and the critical turning points that will occur throughout the time that each of these schools and neighborhoods seeks reinvention of education. Indeed, indigenous invention, a primary concept of the project, would not be working effectively if there were not various differences from school site to school site.

After the diverse stories for each school are told, it will be necessary to examine these stories and identify the common and uncommon properties of the conditions that jointly developed across these project sites. These commonalities and dissimilarities will provide the basis for a better answer to the question "Can it be done?" than any that I can now provide.

I am not naive enough to believe that, at the end of 8 years of project work, a definitive answer to the question will be forthcoming, not because of our inability to find common dimensions to the conditions, but because fundamental reinvention of a social system, such as a school and its surrounding neighborhood, will take longer than 8 years. It is my hope, however, that elements will emerge to help form a foundation for systemic change.

It should be noted that during this time period or any other time frame, neighborhood, community, and national circumstances will shift from year to year, even if in minor ways. When so many societal changes occur, and even though I—and others—have used the existence of such changes to justify educational reinvention, these shifting societal circumstances create a moving target. No one set of invented ideas and practices can adequately address the many changing contextual circumstances that have arisen during the past 5 years, nor can one answer be found for the contextual circumstances that will arise in the future.

Conditions that I might identify as sufficient for promoting reinvention during a given period of project work in the past may not generalize to future contextual circumstances that may arise during a different—but same length of—time in other schools and neighborhoods. Nevertheless, learning about conditions that contribute to a greater understanding of educational change during any given period will contribute to a greater universal understanding of conditions necessary for systemic change.

At this time, the ECC Project can identify a minimum of three conditions that appear necessary to encourage and further promote educational reinvention at Ochoa and the additional school sites. The first clearly grows out of what my colleagues and I have discussed throughout this book:

1. *Advancing Further Dialogue, Inquiry, and Reinvention.* Teachers and the principal of Ochoa have changed their ideas, practices, and structures at Ochoa, yet, even after 5 years, not every aspect of school and classroom work has undergone transformation. Nor do we know sufficiently at this time that the new ideas and altered actions will advance the most powerful knowledge and skills of children in such a manner that Ochoa children will benefit in similar fashion to middle-class children in later years of schooling and beyond.

Because educational reinvention is an ongoing school activity, Ochoa and other schools will engage in continuous dialogue, inquiry, and reinvention at least during the time that they remain connected to the project. What develops in the context of ongoing reinvention in the next few years at Ochoa will further illustrate the potential of reinvention for promoting necessary and sufficient changes in the educational system and add to our insights into the question: "Can it be done?" However, at this time, it is clear that more remains to be done in these areas to more fully answer that question.

The next two conditions draw from the experiences at Ochoa that have become evident to me during the past several years as all of us have responded to the larger educational and community environments that press against the context of an individual school. Seymour Sarason, in *The Predictable Failure of Educational Reform* (1990), has noted that educators pay little explicit attention to the political dimensions of school reform—issues of power and influence—that surround schools and neighborhoods. He suggests that reformers, such as myself, often overlook or underestimate these issues. Consequently, the project focuses attention on—and takes advantage of—what political dimensions can offer, so as not to be done in by them.

2. *The Political Dimensions of Educational Reinvention.* Despite the fact that the ECC Project embraces the school and its neighborhood as the unit of change, the project has and will continue to pay attention to the political dimensions of educational reinvention in the schools, neighborhoods, and beyond. Hence, the project has developed a partnership between the Industrial Areas Foundation/ Southwest, known as the Pima County Interfaith Council (PCIC), to encourage parents and other neighborhood members to identify and seek political action to change certain structural dimensions in their community, that is, better housing, improved community safety, and closer connections between each school and the families and political actions undertaken by neighborhood residents.

Such organizing and political activity promote educational reinvention in two ways. First, both the sense of efficacy among parents and other community members increases, as do the knowledge and skills necessary to identify and solve local neighborhood problems such as adequate housing and the like. This knowledge and these skills among parents and other neighborhood members constitute the social capital that can be promoted among the children and youths of the school and the neighborhood.

Also, as the identification and solution of such neighborhood problems constitute more and more of the contextualized learning for the children (especially in promoting the children in being scientists, mathematicians, etc.), the more directly students acquire ways of thinking and being scientists, writers, mathematicians, and so on, and in identifying and solving complex community problems. In addition, as parents and other neighborhood adults assist in promoting such thinking, the more these adults can promote knowledge and skills and the resulting sense of efficacy among the children in other aspects of community life.

Another future focus of the political dimension of the ECC Project will be assessment of student productions and what these students think about and learn from these productions, as well as judging the worth of the learning opportunities provided by the school. The project is now turning its attention to these assessments, because as this book and other evidence have suggested, many teachers in the school and the principal have altered their thinking and actions in their classrooms and school.

Though other new ideas and practices will continue to arise, the project and participants at the school must now turn their attention to determining the degree to which these new actions do, in fact, promote the most powerful knowledge and skills, making it possible for all Ochoa students to benefit in future years of schooling and beyond.

The ECC Project will promote full participation of parents and other community members in making judgments about the worth of student productions, their thinking and learning about the productions, and the learning opportunities provided by the teachers in the school. If they can see and participate in evidence of students' learning, a public view will be promoted that the students do produce good school work, that they learn and think, and that learning opportunities are worthwhile and connected to student learning and thinking.

In addition, if questions exist among parents and other community members about student productions and learning opportunities provided by the school, participation in such public performances will promote dialogue and inquiry among these community members and the teachers to build shared meanings about the criteria for judging such work. In turn, these adults can then influence the views of others about the quality of what students do and learn in school and the support that the community should or should not provide to the school.

The final political dimension, which the project will promote in the future, focuses on influencing the school district to advocate the new ideas, practices, and structures under way at each project school. Material resources of the school district will have to be reallocated to support these activities and sustain the new ideas and practices that are developed. For example, the new contextualized learning that is developing at Ochoa moves away from decontextualized knowledge and skills usually advocated by most school districts throughout the United States. Material and ideological support exist for acquiring decontextualized knowledge and skills; this support, as well as material resources, will be required to sustain contextualized knowledge and skills. The urging of a large number of parents and local community members for the school district to reallocate resources and support for these project ideas and practices will make the enactment of these practices more likely at Ochoa and ultimately at other schools in the district.

3. *Support and Connections Among Schools and Neighborhoods.* In the 1995-96 school year, the ECC Project will be in five schools and neighborhoods in the Tucson Unified School District. We expanded to these additional sites to gain political influence and colleague support for educational reinvention and to extend the influence and potential of the political aspects previously discussed.

In our future work, we will seek development of support networks for teachers, principals, parents, and district administrators in order to further enhance their understandings and commitments to project ideas and practices discussed in this book. Such networks will support the development of ideas and practices of teachers at project sites and encourage the inclusion of these new ideas and actions in the educational system in Tucson. The many aspects of the ideas and the various practices and structures that can arise in different settings will become evident and be encouraged. In such a support network, variability rather than similarity will be encouraged around a core set of ideas and values underlying the ECC Project.

In summary, we believe that further development and examination of these three conditions will promote a more comprehensive response to the question "Can it be done?" Attention to (at least) these three dimensions will also enhance what some call the systemic reinvention of education in a community such as Tucson, Arizona.

Prospects for the Future

The past accomplishments of the teachers and principal at Ochoa have provided me with great hope that together my colleagues at Ochoa—and at the project's other sites—will sufficiently reinvent education in their communities as well as provide insights into the necessary and sufficient conditions for the ongoing reinvention of education in many other educational settings in the United States.

Given the optimism associated with what I just stated, past experiences with efforts to fundamentally alter the existing educational system suggest that, at the very least, I have to be realistic about the possibility of *fully* reinventing the educational system of a community, the difficulties that will arise in undertaking such an ambitious task, and the potential for what Seymour Sarason has called the predictable failure of school reform.

Finally, I am confident that individuals such as those who have shared their stories in this volume will make every effort to undertake this ambitious task. They have shown their courage and will further exhibit that courage in the months and years to come.

Reference

Sarason, S. (1990). *The predictable failure of educational reform.* San Francisco: Jossey-Bass.

CORWIN
PRESS

The Corwin Press logo—a raven striding across an open book—represents the happy union of courage and learning. We are a professional-level publisher of books and journals for K-12 educators, and we are committed to creating and providing resources that embody these qualities. Corwin's motto is "Success for All Learners."